*J*EWISH ANTECEDENTS
OF THE CHRISTIAN
SACRAMENTS

(1928)

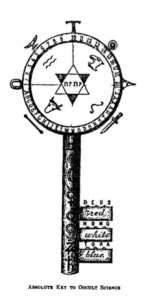

ABSOLUTE KEY TO OCCULT SCIENCE

F. Gavin

THE JEWISH ANTECEDENTS OF
THE CHRISTIAN SACRAMENTS

CHAPMAN LECTURES

THESE chapters were given in substance as lectures in September, 1927, at the S.P.C.K. House, London. They were arranged on the initiative and with the help of Dr. Conrad Chapman and other American friends.

Previously Published

THE JEW AND CHRISTIANITY, by HERBERT DANBY, D.D. Paper cover, 2s. Cloth boards, 3s. 6d

Chapman Lectures, 1926.

THE
JEWISH ANTECEDENTS
OF THE CHRISTIAN
SACRAMENTS

BY

F. GAVIN, Ph.D., Th.D.

PROFESSOR OF ECCLESIASTICAL HISTORY, THE GENERAL
THEOLOGICAL SEMINARY, NEW YORK

LONDON
SOCIETY FOR PROMOTING
CHRISTIAN KNOWLEDGE
NEW YORK AND TORONTO : THE MACMILLAN CO.

IN PIAM MEMORIAM
STANISLAI MATTHEWS CLEVELAND
SACERDOTIS

Obiit die xxvi *Septembris,* MCMXXVI

First Published · · · 1928
Reprinted · · · 1933

PRINTED IN GREAT BRITAIN

SYNOPSIS

LECTURE I (p. 1)

JUDAISM AND SACRAMENTALISM

THE presence of thorough-going sacramentalism in the early strata of the N.T. literature presents the problem, Whence did it come? One answer, recognizing the full weight of the evidence, would point us to non-Jewish mystery-cults as the source of Christian sacramentalism. Another view, minimizing the evidence for primitive sacramentalism, would have us see how largely early Christianity was indebted to Judaism in other respects. Is it possible that early Christian sacramentalism may be traced to Judaism? To this investigation these lectures are addressed. A convenient starting-point may be found in the oft-quoted statement that the Jewish ceremonial rites were not "sacramental" in quality, since they concerned the external only and lacked significance for the life of devotion. (1) It is true that we may not look for a statement or formulation of the sacramental principle in Judaism, both because it was ever reluctant to indulge in theological definition, and (2) because any such definition involves the recognition of the otherness of the "outward and visible," and of the "inward and spiritual." Such terminology operates in a world of thought in which dualistic ideas were current, and while Christian expression utilized the terminology it refused the implications of dualistic ideas. Judaism repudiated such terminology, as is shown by its teaching about God as Creator, its conception of sin in relation to man's liberation from its guilt, the relation of body and soul, and its doctrine of the resurrection of the flesh. (3) The implied contrast between cult acts and religious devotion as of the inner man is utterly foreign to Judaism, which (4) in its essence is radically non-dualistic. (5) In many institutions, as well as implied beliefs, in Judaism the mediation of a changed relationship between God and man was made possible by the use of divinely ordained acts involving

v

material means: the Day of Atonement ceremonial; the
Covenant of Circumcision; the various rites of purification
by immersion or lustration. (6) The use of the Name in the
numerous blessings is also germane to the question, for many
were concerned with sanctifying physical and material objects.
(7) Rudimentary sacramentalism, or at any rate the essential
and germinal factors in sacramentalism, not only existed but
flourished as an essential part of Judaism. In the light of
the above contentions we may feel assured that there is nothing
inherently improbable or impossible in the hypothesis that
Christian sacramentalism was Jewish in origin. The question
then arises, What concrete and specific evidence have we to
indicate that it was?

LECTURE II (p. 26)

JEWISH PROSELYTE AND CHRISTIAN CONVERT

IN the Roman world Judaism possessed the appeal not only
of a religious fellowship characterized by staunch and unswerving loyalty and uncontaminated by paganism, but also
of a monotheism essentially ethical, satisfying both moral and
religious ideals, unswerving in its witness both in practice
and belief, and invested with the power of an ancient and
historic tradition. In his relations with the Gentile the Jew
was often driven to set up barriers to protect the inviolability
of his faith, whether in times of too amicable and therefore
dangerously intimate relations with non-Jewish society, or
in times of persecution. His estimate of Gentiledom is reflected in the ascending climax of his verdict on the Gentile's
susceptibility to contract or communicate "defilement" or
"impurity." The years 150 B.C.–66 A.D. mark the successive
stages of ever more stringent legislation concerning the Gentile.
Intimately bound up with this technical question is that concerning the terms of the non-Jewish proselyte's admission to
the Fellowship of Israel. From before the Christian Era one
part of the convert's admission to Judaism was constituted by
a ceremonial self-immersion—the *tebilah*, or baptism. This
derived from the numerous prescriptions in the Priest's Code.
Of the second or third century we possess two detailed accounts
of the admission of the proselyte to Judaism: in the Tractate
On Proselytes (*Gerim*) and in a Tannaitic memoir in the
Tractate, of the Babylonian Talmud, *On Levirate Marriages*
(*Yebamoth*). An analysis of the contents of these much

abbreviated statements or compends of procedure yields a
sequence of acts and procedure strikingly like that represented in the earliest full account of Christian Baptism—in
the so-called *Egyptian Church Order*. In some cases even the
rubrics are common to the early Christian and contemporary
Jewish usages. Two difficulties remain: the question of the
Christian baptismal formula, and of the agent administering
Christian Baptism. But the Matthæan formula is really in
essence a summary of faith, and self-administered baptism
seems to have been the primitive Christian method. What
as to the changed status and condition of the Jewish Proselyte
and the Christian Convert? What difference was effected by
admission into the religious group? The Rabbinic dictum
that the "newly received proselyte is like a newborn child"
adumbrates the doctrine of baptismal regeneration. In sum,
the fundamental beliefs and practices connected with early
Christian baptism can be accounted for by reference to
Judaism, without recourse to any other factor save the evaluation of Jesus the Messiah by the early Church.

LECTURE III (p. 59)

BERAKHA AND EUCHARIST

ONE of the conspicuous characteristics of Jewish liturgical
prayer has always been the prominence occupied by *thanksgiving*. Innumerable prayers begin with a form of blessing
God. This is conspicuously the case in the forms for grace
at meals: the "blessing of the table" historically included
the use of the Divine Name, the expression of thanks, and the
act of blessing God for the food. The early Rabbinic forms
of such blessings can best be studied in the Common Fellowship Meal ushering in the Sabbath or the Great Feasts. Bread
and Wine had such special and invariable blessings; in these
and all others it was customary unfailingly to use the Name,
though by the first Christian century the ordinary use of
the Name was forbidden, and the order of words prescribed.
The *Berakha* par excellence was for the early Christians the
Eucharist, which term may well have been the attempt to
render the Hebrew noun into Greek. For the explanation of
the origin of the Christian Eucharist we must look rather
to the Fellowship Supper of the Eve (the *Kiddush*) than
to the Passover, and, in order to explain its significance and

unique character, to the early evaluation of our Lord. (1) That
the term Eucharist is intimately bound up with *Berakha* is
suggested strongly by early Christian usage, and *The* Thanksgiving or Blessing was that over the Elements of the Eucharist.
In second-century texts we have curious survivals of the use
of "give thanks" regarded as a transitive verb, effective and
potent to achieve what our Lord enjoined. (2) The indebted-
nesses of early Christian to Jewish liturgical practice are both
significant, abundant, and striking. (3) But the belief and
practice of Judaism cannot fully explain the Christian Eucharist.   The Church's Christology was the chief factor in the
development of eucharistic theology. This must not obscure,
however, the fact that in the light of the Unique Person's
injunction the Eucharist, as unique in its essential character
as was He, never escaped from its certain derivation from
Judaism.

The " Lesser Sacraments " show evidence of their derivation from Judaism, suggested first of all by the high antiquity
of each several rite.   The act of initiation into the Christian
Fellowship comprised a disavowal and repudiation of sin,
Baptism, and the complementary rite of the mediation of the
gift of the Holy Spirit, originally and normally by the imposition of the Apostles' hands.   The whole complex of belief
and practice thus involved concerns intimately the question
of the status of the official ministrant, hence the sacrament
of Orders is bound up with Penance, Baptism, Confirmation,
and the Eucharist.   The official pronouncement of deliverance
from sin, the phenomena known as "speaking with tongues,"
and the character of the early Ministry, all bespeak the
influence of environing Judaism.   Both in the early formulations of Christian marriage regulations and in the rite of
unction, the development of Christian sacramentalism would
seem to have been conditioned by contemporary Judaism.

Primitive sacramentalism may be adequately explained
·by reference to the Judaism of Jesus the Jew, and the conviction that Jesus was much more than a Jew.   The successive stages of nascent sacramental development keep pace
with the growing Christology of the Church.   Never more
than when the debt of Christianity to Judaism is recognized,
does the astounding uniqueness of the evaluation of the
Person of Jesus emerge, as the ultimate basis for the reinter-
pretation of originally Jewish usages into matured Christian
sacramental teaching and practice.

THE JEWISH ANTECEDENTS OF THE CHRISTIAN SACRAMENTS

LECTURE I

JUDAISM AND SACRAMENTALISM

IT seems almost an instinctive craving of the human mind to seek to find the origins of things, and to watch the process of growth from small beginnings. This is eminently true of the story of Christianity. It is equally true of the history of Judaism. But when we come to deal in detail with the findings of modern scholarship in regard to the beginnings of Christianity we discover that students fall roughly into two camps. This alignment is the more clear when it comes to the question of early Christian sacramentalism. One school of thought, popular in Germany, but not without distinguished representatives in the English-speaking world, would have us believe that sacramentalism, early and primitive as it is in the Christian tradition, antedates Catholic or any other kind of Christianity.[1] We are also told to look

---

[1] Cf. K. Lake, *Earlier Epistles of St. Paul*[2], London, 1914, pp. 213 ff. ; *Landmarks in the History of Early Christianity*, London, 1920, pp. 8 ff.

outside Judaism into the ethnic religions, the
" mystery cults," for the origins and parallels of
early Christian sacramentalism. Another school,
which realizes the enormous indebtedness of
Christianity to Judaism—for its Scriptures, its
fundamental beliefs as to God, Creation, the nature
of man, free-will, the Resurrection of the Body,
and what may be called the doctrine of the " true
Israel " [1]—tends to minimize the weight of the
evidence in regard to the sacramental belief and
practice of primitive Christianity. As between the
two we are in an uncomfortable dilemma : the
more emphatically we recognize the primitive
sacramentalism of Christianity the more difficult
it is to reconcile dependence on non-Jewish origins
for the general character of the Church's early
tradition. Or to put it the other way about—when
we see clearly how much Christianity owed to
Judaism we are confronted with the difficult
phenomenon of sacramentalism, so plausibly
explained by recourse to non-Jewish religious cults.

These lectures are addressed to the investigation
of the relationship between early Christian sacramentalism and contemporary Jewish belief and
practice. The upper limit chronologically will be
the close of the Tannaitic period—roughly A.D. 200—
culminating with the authoritative redaction of
the Oral Law in that literature called the Mishna.
It is not to be hoped that final solution or completely
coherent answers may be given to all the problems

[1] Cf. Bonwetsch, " Der Schriftbeweis für die Kirche aus den
Heiden als das wahre Israel bis auf Hippolyt," in *Theologische
Studien Theodor Zahn zum 10ten Oktober* 1908 *dargebracht*,
Leipzig, 1908, pp. 1–22.

presented by our inquiry. The attempt is primarily to present evidence from the Jewish records, indicating in part only and not exhaustively, its pertinence and significance in the light of the developing Christian tradition. Both traditions were far from being fixed in their final form during the first two Christian centuries. The year 200 marks an approximate formulation—by selection and interpretation—of what was then deemed normative. The close of the period saw both traditions in such a form as to condition and largely to control subsequent development. As with Christianity, so with Judaism : much which was deemed irrelevant, inconsistent, and unjustified, found no place in approximate yet authoritative formulations at the beginning of the third century. The very interplay between the two Faiths served to emphasize differences. Hostile rivalry between the two religions would inevitably tend to obscure earlier likenesses in practice and belief, underscore peculiarities on the part of one religion, not shared by the other, and dispense with or discard early traditional usages prone to be misunderstood as indicating perilous similarity with the rival.

At the outset of our investigation, however, we are met with the view widely held and bluntly stated, that what Christianity knows as sacramentalism had nothing like unto it in Judaism. For example, Bousset writes : [1] "Above all, the Jewish Church as a whole knew nothing of sacraments, if by Sacrament we mean a sacred transaction

[1] *Die Religion des Judentums im späthellenistischen Zeitalter*[3], (revised by Gressmann), Tübingen, 1926, p. 199.

in which the believer comes to share in a supernatural gift of grace through material channels."
He goes on to say that the washings and lustrations
of Pharisaism can scarcely have had a sacramental
character, as they were purely external acts
demanded by the Law, possessing only legal and
ceremonial significance, . . . and having " no inner
value for the life of the devout."

If it be true that Judaism had no acquaintance
with what we know as sacramentalism, our investigation will be entirely without point.   But to the
best of my belief these statements are fallacious.
Properly to examine the thesis so crisply asserted
we must proceed to look carefully into the essential
rudiments of a definition of sacrament, draw out
the implications involved, and then turn our attention to the relevant data presented by the Old
Testament as this material survives into Rabbinic
Judaism.   The   discussion   following   may   be
summarized thus :

(1) We cannot rightly expect an explicit
definition or formulation of sacramental thought
in Judaism, as

(2) Current definitions of sacrament, with their
historical ancestry in Christian usage, recognize the
otherness   and   implicit   contrast   (tending   to
opposition) between outer and inner, flesh and
spirit, the material and the non-material, which
is alien to the Jewish point of view.

(3) Yet the implied duality and opposition
between " inner value for the life of the devout "
and outward ceremonial usages is likewise foreign
to Judaism.

(4) Jewish thought and expression was emphatically and radically non-dualistic, almost to the extreme.

(5) In many institutions of Jewish cult may be found the mediation of a changed relationship between God and the Israelite by means of the proper performance of a rite, believed to be divinely ordained, utilizing material means.

(6) The use of blessings and the invocation of the Divine Name therein throws further light upon our subject.

(7) We may conclude that rudimentary and germinal sacramentalism in fact, even if it be not explicitly stated and formulated in theory, not only existed but flourished, as an essential part of the Jewish religion, from the Old Testament into Rabbinism—the orthodox and self-conscious Judaism of the Mishnaic epoch.

To address ourselves to each of these points in turn :

(1) *We may not expect a phrasing or statement of what we call sacramentalism in Judaism.* The Jew was not given to systematic theological formulation. He was not naturally philosophically minded. His religious beliefs and practices were only slowly schematized, and then only under compulsion. It was never congenial to him to formulate theological or philosophical propositions as integral units of a well-planned perspective of thought. His religion—ethical monotheism—of Revelation calling for the response of obedience, was primarily one of conduct and aspiration. It was above all keenly aware of its corporate character. It is

highly significant that no Jewish scholar has ever attempted successfully to write an historical theology of Judaism. The one attempt made by a non-Jewish scholar, Dr. Weber,[1] tried to indicate channels in the uncharted areas of the seas of Rabbinic speculation and meditation. It has been levied upon by all subsequent non-Jewish students who, often to their sorrow, too easily trust the superimposed framework of the author as if it were really knit up with the content. Dr. Weber's work is, of course, extremely inaccurate from the point of view of many of his conclusions. Dr. Schechter,[2] in *Some Aspects of Rabbinic Theology* and his *Studies in Judaism*,[3] and Dr. Kohler in his German [4] as well as his English *Jewish Theology*,[5] have in turn done their best to induce Rabbinic Judaism to yield a system of belief. In this respect their materials did not yield to the attempt, excellent as these two volumes are in other respects. The "creedlessness" of Judaism is a constant puzzle, on the other hand, to Gentile students who find it difficult to conceive of a body of religious belief and practice which is so reluctant distinctly and clearly to define itself.

(2) *Definitions and formulations, foreign to the Jewish tradition, cannot be extracted from it and may not be imposed upon it.* Least of all might we

[1] 1880 ; six years later re-edited as *Die Lehren des Talmud* ; later edition, revised by Schnedermann, *Jüdische Theologie auf Grund des Talmud und verwandten Schriften*, 1897.
[2] New York, 1909.   [3] Philadelphia, 1908, 1911.
[4] *Grundriss einer systematischen Theologie des Judentums auf geschichtlichen Grundlage*, Leipzig, 1910.
[5] "Systematically and historically considered." New York, 1918.

rightly look for a definition of what we term "the sacramental." When we define sacrament as "an outward and visible sign of an inward and spiritual grace . . . ordained by God " we are at once within the realm of characteristically non-Jewish thinking. This succinct statement embodies the recognition of and contrast between, the " outward and visible " and the " inward and spiritual." It is doubtful whether it could have been formulated in a world of ideas in which a dualistic outlook was not at home. Self-conscious Christian thought recognized the distinction, even if it emphatically repudiated the dualism. It came to terms with language even if it declined to endorse the thought. It utilized the premises of dualistic ideology though it refused its conclusions. Now it is extremely important for us to grasp the Jewish outlook as to the universe and its Creator. It may not be without value to turn our attention briefly to the examination of implicit premises in the main current of Jewish religious ideas. Relevant aspects of these ideas concern (a) the ritual and ceremonial conception of sin in the so-called "Priest's Code " and its filiation—evil in relation to God and to man ; (b) the relation of body and soul ; (c) the Law in relation to God and man.

(a) An eminent non-Jewish scholar thus speaks of the primitive rites for purification in the Priest's Code : [1] they " originated in a time when no clear distinction was made between ' uncleanness ' (infringement of a taboo), disease, and moral wrong. . . . In the Jewish laws all these fall under the

[1] G. F. Moore, *History of Religion*, II. New York, 1919, pp. 42-43.

comprehensive name ' sin,' which is at bottom a ritual, not a moral, conception. . . . The sin offering, in the technical use of the term, is not an offering for sin, but for inadvertent transgression of certain ceremonial prohibitions, or is demanded after childbirth, leprosy, the completion of a Nazirite vow, and the like, none of which involve sin, as we understand the word. The result of the inclusion of the moral in the sphere of the religious is that the physical means, efficacious in removing uncleanness, are employed to purify a man from moral defilement or to protect him against the consequences of wrong-doing." The same authority elsewhere describes the process as " physical dis-infection." [1] The phrase to which attention is here particularly called is : " the inclusion of the moral in the sphere of the religious." To the Jew both were one : whether as perverted will or as overt transgression of what Dr. Moore calls a " taboo," all types of such transgression are included under the one heading " sin " ; " the *physical* means efficacious in removing uncleanness are employed to purify a man from *moral* defile-ment." The significance of these words may be illustrated by an incident of a much later time, for the principle survived from the very primitive and early stratum of Jewish religion recorded for us in the so-called " Priest's Code," down into Judaism of the Rabbinic period. During the Maccabean epoch [2] occasions had arisen when Jews

---

[1] " The Rise of Normative Judaism " in the *Harvard Theo-logical Review*, 1924 (XVII.), p. 321.
[2] Sanhedrin 82a ; Aboda Zara 36b.

were contracting illicit and immoral relations with Gentile women. In order to put a stop to this unhappy and scandalous condition the Rabbis had recourse to the expedient, so strange to our thinking, of stigmatizing the relationship as not only " morally " wrong but " ceremonially " wrong, if one may be pardoned the phrase. What we would call a " ritual " proscription was enacted in denouncing such flagrant immorality, and a " ceremonial " ruling was invoked to reinforce the moral law : the Jew so sinning was guilty on four counts, of which the first was that of having intercourse with a woman regarded as in a state of menstrual uncleanness. The Gentile woman, heretofore apparently regarded as outside the scope of the provisions of the ceremonial law, was now to be included within it. That law was now brought into play to prevent moral lapses. Such immorality was thus denounced as " unclean " in what we would call both senses of the word. So far as we know, the expedient operated successfully. By the second century B.C. the inclusion of " moral " and " religious," " ritual " and " ethical," in one sphere was both taken for granted and effectively maintained.

(b) The principle of sin as a communicable infection removable by material means, and its implication that " physical " and " moral " were parts of one larger inclusive whole—survived in Judaism because of its fundamental and characteristic non-dualism. From Genesis through the whole course of Rabbinic literature this is the premise of all deductions. As has been often pointed out, the more painstakingly the early chapters of Genesis

are aligned with contemporary Semitic creation
stories, the more surely does this arresting difference
emerge. The furniture, stage-setting, and scenery
may be shown to be of a piece with other Semitic
folk-lore—but the conclusion and point is glaringly
different : all that is comes from one sole source,
the one and only God. This one unique God, as
self-conscious Jewish monotheism came to see
Him, is He who " kills and makes alive " (Deut.
xxxii. 39), who "forms the light and creates darkness,
who makes peace *and creates evil* " (Isa. xlv. 7).
All things owe their existence to Him, without
exception or qualifications, as all events depend upon
or derive from Him.   As He is one so is His Creation
one.   As creaturedom, of which man is a portion,
is one, so is man—body and soul—a psycho-somatic
unity, one indivisible self.

There is a famous and striking parable, of the
relation between body and soul, told with a view
to the doctrine of the Resurrection. " Antoninus
said to Rabbi : ' The body and soul of a man may
free themselves on the Day of Judgment.' How is
this so ?   The body can say : ' It is the soul that
transgresses, for since I am sundered from it I am
as inert as a stone,' while the soul can say : ' It is
the body that transgresses, for separated from it
I soar like a bird in the air.' "   But Rabbi answered :
" Let me expound a parable which bears on this.
There was once a king who had an excellent garden
of fine figs and set two watchmen over it—of
whom one was blind and the other lame. The
latter said to the former : ' I see some fine figs in the
garden.   Do you take me on your shoulders and

I shall get them for us both to eat.' So it was done and from the back of the blind man the lame man plucked the fruit which both consumed. When later the master of the orchard returned, he found no figs, and to his questions the blind man made answer: ' Have I eyes wherewith to see, that you suspect me of taking the fruit ? ' And after the like manner the lame man : ' Have I feet to go to the fruit ? ' The master then placed the lame man on the back of the blind man and had them both punished together. Thus the Holy One (Blessed be He !) puts back the soul into the body and punishes both together." [1]

Man is thus an indissoluble unity of body and soul, of which each part is essential. Man is neither one nor the other, but both. Sin is of the whole man, not alone either of soul or body. In one theory to account for the existence and universal prevalence of sin among men Rabbinic speculation conceived a curious rival to the Christian doctrine of Original Sin. It stated that man possessed two " impulses " or " urgings," intrinsically indifferent as to moral quality, of which one tended toward good and the other to evil. The moral conflict lies in the struggle to enthrone the good impulse or " urge " over the instinctive impulse of the other one to evil. It is not without significance that Dr. Weber, in his *System der altsynagogalen Palästinischen Theologie*,[2] fell into the seductive error of ascribing the seat of the good impulse (*yeṣer ha-tob*) to the

[1] Sanhedrin 91.
[2] 1880 ; six years later re-edited as *Die Lehren des Talmud ;* later edition, revised by Schnedermann, *Jüdische Theologie auf Grund des Talmud und verwandten Schriften*, 1897.

soul, and that of the evil impulse (*yeṣer ha-ra*) to the body. So attractive was the simplicity of a dualistic solution and so plausibly clarifying its fallacious claim that F. C. Porter's essay,[1] evoked by Weber's misinterpretation of this point of Rabbinic thought, is as significant for its laboured skill in withstanding Weber's thesis as it is distinguished for its detailed and careful rebuttal of a plausible error, and for its careful accuracy as to truth.

(c) As Creaturedom is one, as its Creator, and as man the creature is one, so the Law of God for man is one. Its content is a unity of which no prescription or injunction may be ignored, depreciated, overlooked. From the point of view of nomistic Judaism of the Maccabean epoch and after, the Law, whether in its meticulous directions for lustrations in Lev. xii.–xv. or for the ceremonial of the Day of Atonement (*ibid.* xvi.), is the authentic expression of the revealed will of God. That will takes cognizance of the intimate union between the outward and visible—in short, the material—and the status and position of the individual and community towards God. The two are interdependent. From one point of view " legalistic " Judaism (to use a question-begging term) was highly " materialistic "— in its frank recognition of the place of the material universe in the general scheme of religion. This indictment passed upon Rabbinism frequently rests upon a Manichean premise, as if " material "

---

[1] *The Yeçer Hara : a Study in the Jewish Doctrine of Sin*, in *Biblical and Semitic Studies . . . by the Members of the Semitic and Biblical Faculty of Yale University*, Scribner's, New York, 1902, pp. 91–156.

things were low and degrading, in their essence unworthy of any close intimacy or immediate fellowship with the things of God and the soul. Of that emphasis on a discarnate and immaterial " spirituality " we have sufficient evidence, not only in the depreciation of the robust cognizance of both planes of creaturely life and their incorporation as equals into the frame of the Jewish religious outlook on the world, but in the bias, all too subtly operative, in the case of much Old Testament criticism of a past generation.

(3) *The implied contrast between " inner value for the life of the devout " and outward cult practices*— to hark back to the thought of Bousset—*is* certainly *an alien category*, foreign to anything inherent in Judaism. For example, there is nothing derogatory to the deepest spiritual devotion in a scrupulous adherence to " legalistic " religion. How can one explain the poignantly personal appeal of the Psalter who would find this antagonism between true spirituality and careful observance of " Law " ? From Psalm cxix. to Thomas à Kempis' *Imitation* the coexistence of inward devotion and external " legalism " without any felt inconsistency, should serve as a warning against and a criterion of that ill-regulated confusion of mind which in exalting the spirit would derogate from the dignity of the material. As partners not enemies, the Jew thought of flesh and spirit : as two parts of a whole he thought of " ceremonial " or " ritual " or " legal " and " spiritual." The antonym of spiritual is neither " material " nor " legal " but *un-* or *non-*spiritual.

(4) Just as the inclusion of the moral in the

sphere of the religious seems to have been a per-
plexing phenomenon to the modern student impregnated with a philosophy ultimately due to the
Continental Reformation, so the Jew in his relentless
if unconscious non-dualism would fail to recognize the antithesis always present to the mind of
such present-day scholars, between "legal" and
"religious," "spiritual" and "material," "cult"
and "piety." The whole of religion concerned the
whole of man and was deemed to be a whole
revelation on the part of God which involved a
whole-hearted obedience to Him on the part of the
whole of Israel. God and His expressed will were
concerned with every detail of life, action, and
thought. The view of what we call Nature, of the use
of material things, and of the more material aspects
of physical life was that they all alike spoke for
God, existed by reason of His will, and had, in their
use by man, an intimate connection with that will.

From Psalm xix. to the countless benedictions of
Jewish liturgical devotion, all of the phenomena of
nature were related to God. Nature as such expressed God. Man in using the good things of
this world partakes of God's bounty and sanctifies
the gift in acknowledging it. Social and family life
were alike hallowed by the recognition of the love
of God which made them possible. No feature of
human life lay outside the eternal stream of God's
interest. That in expressing his indebtedness and
voicing his thanks man "sanctified" the world
which he used, is a commonplace in the prayer
forms of Judaism. Normally the "benediction"
began with the words "Blessed art thou, O Lord

God, King of the Universe," whereupon followed the ascription. Sanctification lay close to this eucharistic attitude : the expression of thanks sanctified the gift. The family meal, the annual Passover *seder*, the frequent meetings in fellowship of a group of friends, all adumbrate the Eucharist of Christianity. Nothing in the ordered scheme of Jewish life, lived as under the eye of God, was common or unclean. It was all knit up by dedication, consecration, thanksgiving to the Living One from whom the colourful multiplicity of good things had come.

(5) There are, however, specific rites and institutions of Judaism which still more closely illustrate this principle of the inclusion of all things in the sphere of the religious and the permeation of all things by the divine. In the Priest's Code we have detailed prescriptions for the observance of the Day of Atonement, the annual corporate remembrance of sin and plea for forgiveness. In his *Hibbert Lectures* Montefiore says of the purpose of the ritual of the Day of Atonement that it was " to enable the close relationship between Deity and man to continue undisturbed. The logical circle—that the atoning ceremonies were ordered by God to produce this effect upon himself—was necessarily unperceived by the priestly mind." [1] While this inference is open to further discussion the important element here to be noted is that the rite was believed to be of Divine origin. Whatever significance and efficacy (for both were certainly ascribed to the due performance of the rites) the detailed procedure

[1] Page 337.

possessed, lay solely in the ratification by human obedience of the expressed will of God.

Again, the rite of Circumcision would seem in its solely physical character to be " religiously irrelevant." Its validity and efficacy, its significance and meaning, lay, according to the tradition of Rabbinic Judaism, in its conformity to the explicit will of Deity. More than half a century ago the renowned Jewish scholar Frankel attempted to indicate certain lines of thought relating the Covenant of Abraham to sacramentalism. " Circumcision cannot be quite regarded as a sacrament like Christian Baptism, for in Judaism the principle maintains that by one's birth as a Jew he already belongs to the Community. Yet none the less is it a sacred injunction, which, according to the Talmudic view, is the consummation and realization of all the commandments. Through Circumcision entrance into the fellowship was achieved. It was the son's personal consecration by means of an act established by God, the Sign of the Covenant ordained for all time. Hence Circumcision attained a significance comparable to that of a sacrament. . . . It is the dedication by which the son attains his religious competence." [1] From such an estimate

---

[1] *Zeitschrift für die religiösen Interessen des Judentums*, Berlin, 1844, pp. 66–67. Other scholars have found a sacramental quality in the evaluation of the Covenant of Abraham in Jewish tradition ; *e.g.* Weinel, *Jesus im 19ten Jahrhundert*, 1903, p. 250, justifies the description as " in the truly ancient meaning that through these external media entrance was effected into a moral-supermoral, mystical, and actual relationship with God." Cf. Schlatter, *Die Theologie des Neuen Testaments*, II. p. 497 ; Holtzmann, in *Archiv für Religionswissenschaft*, VII. p. 59 ; Anrich, *Das antike Mysterienwesen in seinem Einfluss auf das Christentum*, Göttingen, 1894, pp. 118 ff. etc.

and interpretation as this it is scarcely a step to a simple assertion that the rite of Circumcision effects and achieves entrance into the proper relationship with God by means of a divinely appointed means.

In connection with this initiatory rite, the Covenant of Abraham, one point of Rabbinical interpretation is of special interest to the student of the early Christian conception of salvation. The injunction of God to Abraham : " Be thou perfect " (Gen. xvii. 1), was taken to mean that circumcision achieved and effected a wholeness and completeness otherwise wanting in man. Full integrity and soundness was to be realized by obedience to the command to circumcise the sons of Israel.[1] It is this same instinct for integrity, completeness, full perfection of body and soul, which seems to lie at the root of the early Christian conception of salvation as *life*, and of Saviour as *Life-giver*.[2] Of the speculations in regard to the effectiveness and value of Circumcision in Rabbinic Judaism, there is no need to speak. It is only here necessary to point out the fact that the rite of Circumcision was deemed to effect a perfection and soundness of man not found in nature, and that the underlying thought of perfectness is closely akin to the primitive Christian conception of salvation as complete life.

In connection with the rites of lustration in

---

[1] In the ancient midrash on Gen. xvii. 1 there is a passage reading : " The Holy One, Blessed be He, said to Abraham : In thee there is naught of blemish save this foreskin. Dispense with it . . . : walk thou before me and thou shalt be perfect " (*Bereschit Rabba*, ed. Theodor, Berlin, 1912, ff. 46: 1, p. 458 ; parallels in notes *loc. cit.*).

[2] Cf. Burkitt, *Early Christianity outside the Roman Empire*, p. 22.

Leviticus—after defilement of various sorts and the like—it is clear that an effect is thought to be achieved by proper performance of the specified rites. In his " unclean " state the Jewish man or woman was in an anomalous situation, removable by material means ordained by God. This quasi-ceremonial, quasi-moral interruption of the normal relationship with God is recognized and provided for in the Law. The same underlying premises operate in the three instances of the Day of Atonement ceremonial, that of the Covenant of Abraham, and the rites of purification : material means are adequate and mandatory agencies for the restoration of the divinely-willed status of the individual Israelite towards his God and his Community.

It is further to be noticed that in every single instance the emphasis is laid upon the supposed divine authorization for the rite or usage in question. God is pleased *in this way* to effect the end in view. This principle is of immense importance as foreshadowing matured Christian sacramental belief, for it sharply distinguishes these ceremonial and objective acts from the essential characteristic of magic. We are overwhelmed to-day by a steady and consistent stream of propaganda which would induce or coerce us to recognize in all utilizations of the material for religious, ceremonial, or ritual ends, the existence and presence of magic and superstition. This type of argument is plausible and apparently convincing until we delve into definitions in an attempt to clear the issue. There is, of course, no question that primitive religion as well as primitive science—or the ancestor of what we later call science—are as closely akin as are both to what the modern world is pleased to term magic and superstition. The sense that to inadequate causes are ascribed cogent and potent effects, is part of what we mean by superstition. So far as interpretation of a given set of phenomena be concerned, our use of the term superstition is both a begging of the question and in essence a value-judgment.

How shall we define *magic* ? We may not deem it sufficient to describe it as a utilization of a formula, rite, or ceremony in order to produce phenomena utterly incommensurate with, or and surpassing the power of, the cause. The heart of the matter lies still deeper, for it concerns the aim and purpose of the use of the formula we should call " magical." For example, the story of Aladdin and the jinns is a tale of pure magic. What is the essential factor in the case ? Is it not the power possessed and exercised by Aladdin of coercing forces, ordinarily outside the range of his control, by means of the technique called " magical," to do his will ? In each instance of what may be alleged to be magic this fundamental characteristic maintains : the person in possession of the magical secret can impose his will on others, without reference to their desires. The broadly-defined type of primitive religion that can be called magical presents the same character-istic : the person employing the proper method can disarm the hostility or opposition of a supernatural power, even of the Deity, and coerce it to do his will. As to the salient quality of magic we may then say that it consists in the imposition of the will of the person possessing the secret on that of another, whether human or other-than-human, by the use of some formula or rite having this coercive power.

How, then, do the rites of Judaism or the sacraments of Christianity fare when measured by this definition ? To take the more extreme case : does not the scholastic definition of the operation of the sacramental principle, in terms of the doctrine of *ex opere operato*, fall under this indictment ? At first glance it would surely seem so : the proper person, with due intention, the proper form and matter, and lo, the bread and wine are transubstantiated into the Body and Blood of Christ ! Yet as one looks under the surface, two profound facts emerge in the consideration of what might be termed extreme sacramental doctrine : (1) the sacraments have their sole excuse for being in what is deemed to be explicit divine injunctions for their institution and continuance. So there is certainly no advantage taken of Deity, nor any imposition of human will on His—but the precise reverse : all that is done is done because it is believed to be His Will that is being carried out. (2) What of the worshipper ? If the sacraments are consummated *ex opere operato*, do they not function irrespective of the will of the human persons concerned ? The distinction between *res sacramenti* and *virtus sacramenti* may, in respect to this phase of the discussion, be reduced to the simple statement : sacramental efficacy so far as concerns the individual subject is precluded if there be obstructive will on his part. So upon examination the accusation that matured and extreme sacramental views are essentially magic, falls to the ground completely.

What saves both Christian sacramentalism and the ceremonial and ritual practices of Judaism from any tinge or taint of the magical is the strong conviction of the divine authorization of these rites. God is being obeyed by man's fulfilment of His terms, and in obedience to the divine injunction His will is being carried out.   As a matter of fact, before the destruction of the Temple Rabbinic thought had explored the other side of the question as well, and had come essentially to the same conclusion as is represented, *cæteris paribus*, by the scholastic distinction mentioned above : the efficacious operation, as far as concerns the individual of the prescribed Day of Atonement ceremonial, was conditioned by the subjective attitude of the worshipper.[1]   In the light of this approach to the difficulty the Rabbis and the Schoolmen seem to have come to the same type of solution.   In the larger issue it must be remembered that for both religions the sole essential justification of the rites lay in the conviction that in performing them the expressed will of God was being scrupulously obeyed.

Of course, there is little consideration of the subjective factor in the early strata of the Jewish tradition.   The chief concern of the redactor was with the due performance of the objective rite itself.   Little account is taken or recognition made of the inner attitude or disposition of the individual,

[1] Cf. Sheb. I. 6 ; Yoma VIII. 8, 9, etc. ; and cf. Schechter, *Some Aspects of Rabbinic Theology*, pp. 293 ff.

for the " individual " was not as yet fully discovered, and the due performance of the rite might be taken as evidence of proper disposition. Prophetic religion did enormously affect the main stream of Judaism. The messages of repentance and conversion of heart found their place in the fully self-conscious religion of Rabbinism.

(6) In passing, it may be well to allude to the use of the Divine Name in invocation, in the numerous prayers and benedictions in use in Judaism. Grace at meals was the explicit recognition of the gift of God in creaturedom. " God saw that it was good " was the basis of the blessings. The invocation of the Name (cf. Jer. vii. 14 ; xiv. 9b, etc.) has been studied by Heitmüller in his brilliant essay, *Im Namen Jesu*, who concludes that it was deemed to convey, achieve, and release Divine Power.[1] The use of His Name, approved and enjoined by God, made effective that which it expressed. The use of the Name and its significance in Jewish blessings will be more fully discussed in Lecture III.

(7) In the light of these considerations it would seem that there is nothing inherently improbable in assuming that Judaism furnished the materials for Christian sacramentalism. It is clear that we may not expect an explicit sacramental doctrine in Judaism, because of the reluctance of Judaism to define and state the principles of its beliefs, and because the very phraseology of sacramental statement belongs to an un-Jewish environment. Furthermore, the distinctions between " natural "

[1] Göttingen, 1903, pp. 132–154 ff. ; pp. 171–176, etc.

and " supernatural," " ceremonial " and " religious,"
" material " and " spiritual," " legalism " and
" piety " do not belong to the tradition of Judaism,
and it is difficult to express, interpret, or discuss
sacramentalism without recourse to these terms,
which happened to be congenial to the world of
nascent Gentile Christianity. But in failing to
discover the theory, we are not justified in denying
the fact : the essential germinal principles of a
sacramental outlook on the universe were not only
tolerated by Judaism, but even lay intimately at
its centre. A sound Christian definition of sacrament proceeds from the characteristically Jewish
premise that the material world is not evil, but good
—since God made it and saw it to be good.

This premise was further reinforced in Christianity
by the doctrine of the Incarnation and by that of the
Holy Spirit : (a) In the Incarnation God found a
material human body no unfit vehicle by which to
express the Divine, and all of human nature, in-
dissolubly body and soul, was caught up into juxta-
position and intimate union with Deity. (b) In
the matured doctrine of the sacraments the Holy
Spirit is believed to utilize material channels as
means of grace. So matter is triply sanctified—in
origin as from God, in the Incarnation, and in the
Dispensation of grace. With the Jewish doctrine
of the Resurrection of the Flesh, taken over by
Christianity, we have further evidence of the point
of view common to it and Judaism.

If a sacrament be defined as " the outward and
visible sign of an inward and spiritual grace . . .
ordained by God " we have in the definition formally

exceeded the boundaries of the characteristic world of Jewish ideas. But all these elements were present in Judaism : the utilization of material means to initiate, achieve, reconstitute, or maintain the proper relationship between man and God ; the primitive conception that " sin " can be done away by material means ; the ascription of effective power to the rites and ceremonies thus employed, as being specifically ordained and enjoined by the God of nature and of grace, and the investigation, if somewhat inchoate and rudimentary, of the necessary subjective conditions on the part of man in order for the divinely-commanded rite efficaciously to attain its end in the case of the individual. The phraseology of the Christian definition of sacrament is un-Jewish ; the essential factors which that definition comprises are all present in Judaism. The transition which Christianity experienced from being a Jewish sect into becoming a universal and chiefly non-Semitic Church [1] developed acutely certain problems which were entirely foreign to Judaism, with its un-dualistic outlook embracing, in one ordered whole, man as body-spirit, religion as cult and inward piety, ethics as intimately conjoined with religion, the secular as inseparable from the religious, and God's will as above all yet concretely applicable to every act of every man's life and thought at every point.

Having sketched in outline certain preliminary

[1] It must not be forgotten that while we generally recognize two large types of Catholic Christianity—Greek and Latin—there were, for some four centuries and more, three : Semitic Catholicism, with its Syriac literature (best represented by Aphraates the Persian Sage), has practically disappeared.

considerations in the light of which the derivation
of Christian sacramentalism from Judaism may not
seem to have been inherently improbable or
essentially impossible, let us turn to the examination
of concrete evidence.   Are there any positive data
which suggest a direct relationship between Judaism
and early Christian sacramental belief and practice ?

LECTURE II

THE first-century world was intensely interested
in " religion." In the efforts to rejuvenate
the established religion of the Empire, political
loyalty, patriotism, and the sense of imperial self-
consciousness were all invoked by those in authority
to reinvigorate Roman paganism. While the
educated Roman of culture and idealism was undoubtedly thereby little satisfied religiously, he could
be, as he was, solaced by the quasi-religious systems
of later Platonism, Stoicism, and Epicureanism.
Upon the many, the mystery cults probably exercised a strong influence. The ethnic religions
of conquered peoples survived only by undergoing
a radical transformation as was almost invariably
the case, they had begun as national or tribal
religious, the apotheosis of race loyalty, membership in which was constituted by birth. They had
to suffer a vast alteration in order to maintain
themselves, when their old national character was
brought to an end by the series of conquests from
Alexander the Great on to those successes of
the Roman Republic. The essential changes
involved were, first, they advanced the claim to be

26

universal rather than national, tribal, or racial ; secondly, they became soteriological by means of a new interpretation of their several rites ; thirdly, they changed the basis of their membership, by addressing their propaganda to adult potential converts led by conviction and choice to membership, rather than by enrolling all born within a given territory. A further note of these cults was their syncretism. As none did nor could claim to be sole and unique, each was compelled to adjust itself to living with others, within the large, tolerant comprehensiveness of Roman religious hospitality.

It is precisely in the last particular that Judaism showed itself so distinct and different. The Jewish State had come to an end long before most of those ethnic groups whose religions survived into the Roman world as mystery cults. The message of the prophets had purged Judaism of any tincture of monolatry ; the God of the Jew was perceived to be the only God there was. While the racial or nationalistic factor was never fully to be submerged it did not lessen the appreciation of the unique character of the God of all the universe. The implications of self-conscious monotheism entailed in principle effort for the conversion of all mankind to perceive the necessity of worshipping Him, as the One and only God, whom the Jews had always revered. The Jew enjoyed a high degree of religious freedom under Roman rule. His rights, privileges, and peculiarities were respected. His might be one only of the many religions tolerated by the Government, but it was not demanded that he compromise his convictions. The Jew sedulously

and steadily declined to conciliate the spirit of
tolerance and broad-mindedness by abating one
jot his conviction of the dogmatic certitude of the
unique and universal character of his God and of
God's Revelation. He could not be a syncretist.
He was, as now, highly adaptable to external
conditions and his cultural environment. But
from the standpoint of the Pagan world without
he was bitterly and offensively intolerant. At no
time would he feel at ease in a society where religion
and morality were divorced ; he was not comfortable
in a life in which he always viewed with alarm the
contaminating influences of close contact with
heathen society. Almost in direct proportion to
his restiveness under conditions of social intercourse, fraught with grave danger to the precious
values of religion, he withdrew into exclusive
aloofness, and at the same time, furthered without
cessation his propagandist efforts to win Gentiles
to the acknowledgment of One God and obedience
to His expressed will.

There are many aspects of Jewish propagandist
activities which are lost in the silence of our sources.
It is only by piecing together scattered references,
chiefly in the literature of the Tannaitic period (the
first two centuries of the Christian Era), that we
can provisionally reconstruct and tentatively infer
the probable facts. All men should acknowledge
the one and only God who had revealed His will to
the Jew. The privilege of the Jew involved the
responsibility of proclaiming this message, as well as
of living and conducting his own life in accordance
with the Divine Revelation. The Gentile world

was always a danger : in times of peace and
prosperity danger lurked in the specious security
of amicable relations between the Jew and his
non-Jewish neighbours, dulling the edge of the
Jew's religious convictions, lulling him to a false
optimism, and subverting the poignant affirmations
of his faith. In times of sporadic persecution or
active hostility on the part of the Gentile world,
the dangers were apparent and obvious : yet the
Jew must never preserve his own life by a sacrifice
of his faith. The more easy and comfortable the
relations between Jew and Gentile in times of peace,
the more likely a gradual deterioration and progressive debilitation on the part of the Jew, to be
manifested in the event of persecution. So we find
that at times of too great intimacy barriers were
raised against intercourse with Gentiles, to be
scaled up still higher and more sharply affirmed in
times of strained relations.

We have already alluded to the curious bit of
legislation enacted in the Maccabean epoch, to put
a stop to immoral relations between Jews and Gentile
women. We noted above that the Rabbis ruled
that a Jew thus sinning was guilty on four counts,
among them, that of having intercourse with a
woman whose condition was stigmatized as constantly unclean with the uncleanness attaching to
menstruation (A. Z. 36b ; Sanhedrin 82a). What
the implications of this ruling are must occupy our
attention at this point. As Büchler has pointed out
in his excellent essay,[1] Gentile women presumed
to be so unclean would have to submit to a puri-

[1] *Jewish Quarterly Review*, July, 1926, p. 15.

ficatory bath or *tebilah*, if they were becoming
proselytes to Judaism. A second implication is
that to the male Gentile, born of a woman thus
unclean, would attach a derivatory and secondary
degree of uncleanness. The ruling may well have
lapsed by the beginning of the first century A.D.,
yet the evidence collected by Büchler suggests
that it was still in effect at that time. In the
troublous years preceding the Fall of the Temple in
A.D. 70 the spirit of this type of legislation was
revived, and successive restrictive measures enacted
against Gentiles, to the end of precluding all social
contacts whatever. In the famous " Eighteen
Proscriptions " we find this sort of enactment
culminating in the dictum that the " Gentile is in
all respects like a man with an unclean issue," [1]
in other words, he is regarded as unclean in the
highest degree. It must, however, be kept in
mind that along with this tradition had coexisted
another, quite inconsistent with it : that the non-
Jew was by nature unsusceptible of contracting
uncleanness, as the obligations of observing the
laws of clean and unclean were not incumbent upon
him. It would take us too far afield to attempt to
reconcile or adjust these two traditions. The fact
that the former was operative antecedent to the rise
of Christianity is sufficient for our purpose, to illumin-
ate that method of initiating proselytes to Judaism
which is commonly called Proselyte-Baptism.

An explicit reference to this rite is to be found
in Mishna Pesaḥim VIII. 8, where the recipients

---

[1] Cf. A. Z. 36b ; also Nidda 34b ; Sifra to Lev. xv. 2 (74d) ;
Tos. Zab. II. 1 (Zuckermandel, p. 677).

are non-Jewish soldiers. Toward the end of the first or beginning of the second century R. Joshua and R. Eliezer ben Hyrkanos could debate whether Baptism or Circumcision be the essential rite of initiation into Judaism (Yebamoth 46a). Pharaoh's daughter, we are told, went down to the river " to wash off the defilement of her heathen descent " (Sotah 12b). From the first century on, references to Proselyte-Baptism are numerous. That it could be a matter of debate by the end of the first century suggests definitely that it had been a long prevailing practice, and the incident alluded to in Pes. VIII. 8 reinforces the inference of proscriptive use of a much earlier date. When the authorities of the Talmud have to deal with this Mishna their recorded opinions show how the clue to the origin and significance of the rite lay outside their ken.

The Baptism of Proselytes would be an obvious and natural procedure. The Law prescribed an immersion-bath for purification in a dozen instances. A state of defilement or uncleanness had to be removed by complying with a divinely ordained ceremony, as a means of rehabilitation to the normal state of cleanness, " moral " as well as " ceremonial " (to use these question-begging terms !). What, then, was the rite of Proselyte-Baptism ? What was the significance of the change from heathenism to Judaism ?

Our sources are two, and neither gives the rite in its fullness. One is imbedded as a Tannaitic reminiscence in the Babylonian Talmud (Yeb. 47). Another is found in a curious little manual *On Proselytes (Gerim)*, which is one of the " extra "-

canonical Tractates of the Talmud. This Tractate
would seem to be a handbook of Palestinian usage,
compiled from early material, and redacted at a
later time primarily for the purposes of record.
The underlying framework of the rite is the same
in both accounts, but there are divergences. Apart
from rubrics the rite thus recorded consists of the
following parts : (a) The presentation and examination of the Candidate ; (b) the instruction of the
Candidate ; (c) his circumcision if a male ; (d) the
act of Baptism—entering the water, summary
résumé of some elements of the instruction, the
act of immersion (and a final address of congratulation and exhortation). Both accounts, in their
compression and succinctness, need to be supplemented from scattered details found elsewhere in
early Rabbinic literature. These are noted below.
It is not possible in these lectures fully to discuss
the problem of the date of the contents of the rites
here recorded. It is, on the whole, most probable
that the rite as here described is that of the early
half of the second century. Peculiar to the account
in *Gerim* are the words : " (the Jews) are put to
death for Circumcision, Baptism, and all the other
Ordinances," which best fit a date soon after the
Bar Kokheba uprising and the ensuing Synod of
Usha (*circa* A.D. 135–140).[1]

[1] Cf. also Büchler, *Der galilaische 'Am ha-'ares*, pp. 6–7 and
note. The Synod of Usha prescribed a court of three *ḥaberim* ;
cf. Tos. Dem. II. 13 ; Yer. Dem. II. 22d ; Bekh. 30b ; A. Z.
64b ; and the accounts in Gerim I. 2–5, Yeb. 47b, etc. The
baraitha in A. Z. 64b, which deals with the *ger toshab*, defines
him as " one who *in the presence of three ḥaberim* forswears
idolatry," and the same passage lacking, however, the italicized
words appears in Gerim III. 1.

The two accounts in parallel follow:

YEB. 47a.	GERIM I.

A. Presentation and Examination of Candidate.

One who comes to be made a proselyte in the present time is to be asked: "Why dost thou come to be made a proselyte? Dost thou not know that at this time Israel is afflicted, buffeted, humiliated and harried, and that sufferings and sore trials come upon them?" If he answer: "I know this, and am not worthy," they are to accept him immediately.	1. One who desires to be made a proselyte is not to be received immediately, but they are to ask him: "What makes thee desire to become a proselyte? Behold, seest thou not how the People is humbled and afflicted among the nations of the world, how many ills and sufferings come upon them, how they bury their sons and grandsons, and how they are put to death for Circumcision, Baptism, and all the other Ordinances, and do not conduct their lives openly and freely like all the other peoples?" 2. If he answer: "I am not worthy to give my neck to the yoke of Him Who spake the word and the world came into existence," they are to accept him immediately. If not, he is dismissed and goes on his way.

B. The Instruction of the Candidate.

Then they are to instruct him in some of the lighter and some of the weightier commandments; and inform him as to the sins in regard to the *corner of the field, the forgotten sheaf, the gleaning, and the tithe for the poor.* Then shall they teach him the penalties for transgression: "Know well that up until the time that thou hast come hither thou hast eaten the forbidden fat of cattle without incurring the sentence of excommunication;	(Cf. 1 : 3, under D.)

YEB. 47 a, b.   GERIM 1.

that thou hast profaned the
sabbath without incurring the
penalty of lapidation. But
from now on if thou eat the
forbidden fat of cattle thou
wilt be excommunicated ; if
thou profanest the Sabbath
thou wilt be stoned." In the
same way as they instruct
him about the penalties of
transgression shall they teach
him the rewards for observance
of the commandments and
shall say to him : " *Know thou*   (Cf. 1 : 5 below, under D.)
that the world to come was made
only for the righteous, but
Israel at this present time
may not experience very great
good or very great afflictions
(47b). Yet one must not
multiply words or go too
much into detail.

C. Circumcision.

If he accept, he is to be   3. In case he assume (the
circumcised immediately and   obligation) upon himself
received. In case of the dis-
covery of any defect as to (a
previous) circumcision, he is
to be circumcised over again,
and when healed brought to   they bring him down to the
baptism immediately.   baptistery,

D. Baptism.

Two men learned in the   and cover him with water to
Law shall stand near him and   his genitals. They recite to
instruct him as to some of the him certain particular com-
lighter and some of the   mandments : that he should
weightier commandments.   begin to give the corner of the
                               field, the forgotten sheaf, the
                               gleaning, and the tithe.
                                   4. As they instruct a man,
                               so they instruct a woman :
                               that she should begin to be
                               scrupulous in regard to the

YEB. 47b.   GERIM I.

regulations as to purification, the priest's share of the dough, and the kindling of the Sabbath light.

He immerses himself and when he comes up he is in all respects an Israelite.

5. He immerses himself, and when he comes up they address him (with) " comforting words " :

E. ADDRESS OF CONGRATULATION.

" To whom thou hast joined thyself ? Happy (art) thou ! To Him who spake the word and the world came into existence, for the world was created only for Israel's sake,[1] nor are there any called ' sons ' save Israel, and all the words which we spake unto thee we have said only in order to increase thy reward."

RUBRICS.

Women place the woman (proselyte) in water up to her neck and two sages shall stand without near-by, and instruct her as to some of the lighter and some of the weightier commandments.

The same rule prevails for a woman taking her bath of purification after the *menses* as for the case of a proselyte and for that of a slave attaining his freedom : they immerse themselves and whatever is a precluding impediment by reason of a " separating element " (*ḥoṣeṣ*) maintains for all three cases alike.

(Cf. 1 : 4 above, under D.)

I. 8. Men baptize men and women baptize women, but women (do not baptize) men.

(Cf. also 1 : 6, 7.)

[1] Cf. the *Shepherd of Hermas, Vis.* II. 4: " The Church is old, and for her sake was the world established."

Certain supplementary details may be added from other sources, chiefly Tannaitic :

(a) The provision that the master, at the Proselyte-Baptism of his slave, must retain his hand upon him (cf. Yeb. 46a) *may* reflect a Tannaitic custom at the rite. Possibly one of the official witnesses did so in the case of the convert, in which case his hand would go under the water too, to avoid invalidating the rite by reason of an " element of separation " (*ḥoṣeṣ*) (Mikwaoth VIII. 5).

(b) The benediction to be recited after *tebilah* is given in Pes. 7b : ." Blessed art thou who didst sanctify us by thy commandments and has enjoined upon us the *tebilah*."

(c) The benediction at the circumcision of a convert is given in Sabbath 137b as follows : " He who circumcises a proselyte says : ' Blessed art Thou, O Lord our God, King of the Universe, who didst sanctify us by thy commandments and enjoin upon us Circumcision.' He who recites the benediction says : ('Thou who didst) sanctify us by thy commandments and enjoined us to circumcise proselytes and to extract from them (him) a drop of the blood of the Covenant, for were it not for the blood of the Covenant heaven and earth would not maintain.' "

(d) Provisions against clandestinity : (1) The necessity of witnesses, mentioned above, which regulation, apparently after Usha, meant *three* sages (cf. Yeb. 46b–47a, and Kidd. 62a–b). In Gerim IV. 3 occur the words : " Beloved of God is the land of Israel for it facilitates proselytism. If one say, inside Palestine : ' I am a proselyte,' he

is to be received immediately ; but outside Palestine
he is not received unless there be witnesses with
him." The lengthy debate between Tannaim in
Yeb. 47a on the subject of producing proof illus-
trates the sense of need for authentication of the
admission of a proselyte as having been duly performed. (2) The prohibition of Proselyte-Baptism
by night (Yer. Yeb. VIII. 1 (8d) and Yeb. 46b).
The Tannaitic consensus specifies daytime.

(e) The *tebilah* had to be of " living water," if
possible, and sufficient in quantity to allow of
complete immersion of the body. The mention
of " living water " in the Torah (Lev. xiv. 5, 50–52 ;
xv. 13 ; Num. xix. 17) is the ultimate source for
the extension of the principle concerning it to certain
of the purificatory baths. The treatise Mikwaoth
of the Mishna deals with the quantity and character
of the water used for such purposes. Apparently
the difference of opinion between Bet Hillel and
Bet Shammai as to the quantity of " artificial "
(=drawn) water which invalidates a purificatory
bath (cf. Sab. 15a) postulates the existence of the
Rabbinic distinction between it and living water.
If the date of the debate be—as Lerner [1] puts it—
the middle of the first century, we have a datum
for the distinction and prescription of " living
water." But in his stimulating and acute essay,
*Die rituellen Reinheitsgesetze in der Bibel und im
Talmud*, Dr. Katzenelson argues very plausibly for
a date in the Persian period for the specification
of immersion (as against Persian aspersion) in living

---

[1] *Magazin für die Wissenschaft des Judentums*, 1885, p. 113.

water,[1] and points out that the abrogation of the immersion for purification of the man who had experienced nocturnal pollution was enacted during the latter part of the first century.[2]   The Mishnaic evidence as to the character and quantity of the water (" enough to cover the whole body," Ḥag. 11a) is to be construed in the light of this background.[3] It is safe to assume that the proselyte's baptism was by immersion in living water.   As Abrahams writes : " It seems to me that there is no adequate ground for doubting that Jewish baptism in the first century was by total immersion." [4]

The words in Gerim I. 5, " all that we have said unto thee," etc., postulate a more lengthy and detailed instruction of the convert than has found explicit mention in the text, and the section in Yeb. 47 leaves so much to inference that in both cases we may feel assured that some sort of systematic instruction had taken place.   We cannot rest satisfied with the conclusion that the observances specifically noted in these accounts comprised the whole content of the instruction.   What, then, was this traditional teaching which constituted the

---

[1] Cf. Part V. in *Monatsschrift für die Geschichte und Wissenschaft des Judentums*, 1900 (44: 10), pp. 433–451.

[2] Cf. Part V. in *Monatsschrift für die Geschichte und Wissenschaft des Judentums*, 1900 (44: 10), pp. 446–447 ; cf. Ber. 22a.

[3] It is ably marshalled by Abrahams, " How did the Jews baptize ? " in *J.T.S.* XII. (1911), pp. 609–612 ; vs. C. F. Rogers, *J.T.S.* XII. (1911), pp. 437–445; and XIII. (1912), pp. 411–414, with which may be compared Lauterbach in *J.E.* VIII. pp. 587–588 ; Abrahams, *Studies in Pharisaism and the Gospels*, First Series, Cambridge, 1917, pp. 38–40 ; W. Brandt, *Die jüdische Baptismen oder das religiöse Waschen und Baden im Judentum mit Einschluss des Judenchristentums*, Giessen, 1910, especially pp. 46 ff. etc.

[4] *J.T.S.* XII. p. 612.

proselyte's instruction ? There have been attempts to deal with this question in works which have concerned themselves with proselytism.[1] A. Seeberg's contentions represent a conservative conclusion based on the examination of the pertinent evidence. He finds [2] that the content of the Jewish convert's instruction was triple : dogmatic, ethical, and eschatological,[3] which he seeks to restore by analysis of the material available [4] and then proceeds to deal with the *Didache* and the history of the catechetical material in the first century.[5] Despite the vagaries of Klein's book [6] the author has performed a great service in calling attention to the *derekh 'eres* literature as a possible repository for instructional material, and in his

---

[1] Felsenthal, *Zur Proselytenfrage im Judenthum*, Chicago, and Breslau, 1878, pp. 1–47 ; *ibid.* in Frankel-Graetz *Monatsschrift*, xxvii. (1878), pp. 236–240 (where he has an interesting discussion of the debate between R. Joshua and R. Eliezer in Yeb. 46) ; N. Samter, *Judenthum und Proselytismus*, Breslau, 1897, pp. 1–40 ; F. Sieffert, *Die Heidenbekehrung im A.T. und im Judenthum*, Berlin, 1908, pp. 1–48 ; I. Weil, *Le prosélytisme chez les Juifs selon la Bible et le Talmud*, Strassbourg, 1880, pp. 1–109 ; Juster, *Les juifs dans l'empire Romain*, Paris, 1914, I. pp. 290–304 ; Encyclopedia articles, *s.v.* " Proselyte," etc. Specifically Kohler (*JE* IV. pp. 585–588) ; A. Seeberg, *Der Katechismus der Urchristenheit*, Leipzig, 1903 ; *ibid., Die beiden Wege und das Aposteldekret*, 1906 ; and *ibid., Die Didache des Judentums und der Urchristenheit*, 1908 ; and G. Klein, *Der älteste christliche Katechismus und die jüdische Propaganda Literatur*, Berlin, 1909, have dealt with the form and content of this instruction, as have all the editors of that interesting document, *The Didache, or the Teaching of the Twelve Apostles*, from Taylor (Cambridge, 1886) ; Harnack, *Die Apostellehre und die Jüdischen zwei Wege*, Leipzig, 1895 ; and Rendell Harris, *The Teaching of the Apostles*, London, 1887 ; to Knopf, *Die apostolischen Väter 1. Die Lehre der zwölf Apostel*, Tübingen, 1920

[2] *Die Didache*.
[3] *Ibid.* pp. 1–5.
[4] *Ibid.* pp. 1–69.
[5] *Ibid.* pp. 83–100.
[6] *Der älteste christliche Katechismus.*

commentary on the *Didache*,[1] has assembled many
suggestive and significant data.

It is impossible to make any résumé of the conclusions of those who have dealt with the question,
but on the assumption that the general thesis is
sound we may see reflections and hints of just this
type of instruction in the bald summary given in
Yeb. 47 (" lighter and weightier commandments,"
" penalties for transgressions," " the world to come
was made only for the righteous," etc.) as well as
in Gerim I. (2 : " give my neck to the yoke of Him
who spake the word and the world came into
existence "—cf. Mk. x. 15 ; *ECO*, Horner, *op. cit.*
p. 160 ; Ber. VI. 3 ; 3 : " particular prescriptions
of the commandment " ; 5 : the " comforting
words," etc.). The phrase, " All these words have
we spoken unto thee only to increase thy reward "
(Gerim I. 5) are parallel to the resumptive phrase
in *Didache* VII. 1, ταῦτα πάντα προειπόντες,
introducing the directions as to baptism.[2]

Any discussion of the place of baptism in the
belief and practice of early Christianity must needs
take into cognizance the general theories and conclusions of the scholars who deal with it. There
have been those who would minimize the Evangelical
and Epistolary references to it, depreciating their
significance and reducing it to the vanishing point.
Others of a more recent school would see in it con-
clusive evidence, present throughout the structure
and thought of primitive Christianity, of the

[1] *Der älteste christliche Katechismus*, pp. 184–238.
[2] Knopf, *op. cit.* p. 2 : *Als sicher kann gelten dass in Did.
1–6, eine ursprünglich jüdische Schrift, die " beiden Wege,"
verarbeitet ist.*

influence of a sacramentalism derived from the mystery cults. Probably in such essay as Von Stromberg's *Studien zur Theorie und Praxis der Taufe in der' christlichen Kirche der ersten drei Jahrhunderte*, Berlin, 1913, we can best find the relevant material presented and expounded. A few remarks on the evidence of the N.T. will have to suffice, before we turn our attention to the material contained in early Christian literature outside the Bible. One outstanding fact is clear. In the N.T. tradition, the place of John the Baptist is of great importance. When our Lord was asked for evidence of His authority He asked in return the question, whether the baptism of John were from heaven or from men.[1] St. Peter's speech (Acts x. 37) dates the Christian Gospel as "beginning from Galilee after the baptism which John preached," and in Acts i. 5 occur the words : "For John indeed baptized with water, but ye shall be baptized with (the) Holy Spirit. . . ." In Acts ii. 38 : "Peter said unto them, Repent ye, and be baptized every one of you in the name of Jesus Christ unto the remission of your sins, and ye shall receive the gift of the Holy Spirit," and St. Luke iii. 3 describes John as "preaching the baptism of repentance unto the remission of sins." [2]

In the N.T. two primary conceptions are bound up with baptism : one negative—the washing away of sin and guilt, the cleansing from evil, often expressed as "death unto sin," and the other

[1] St. Mark xi. 30 ; St. Matt. xxi. 25 ; St. Luke xx. 4.
[2] Cf. St. Mark i. 4 ; Acts i. 22 ; v. 31 ; x. 43 ; xiii. 38 ; xxii. 16 ; xxvi. 18 ; St. Luke i. 77 ; xxiv. 47, etc.

D

positive—the new status with God and the Fellowship, regarded as regeneration, new birth, a " new
creation," or as " life unto righteousness."   To the
writer of Acts,[1] baptism and the reception of the
Holy Spirit normally ought to be intimately conjoined, despite such anomalies as are represented
by the reception or co-option of Apollos.[2] The
N.T. contains neither a complete theory nor an
explicit rite for the administration of baptism. For
the former we must wait for years to pass in the
development of Christian belief ; for the latter we
may turn to such early manuals of practice as are
represented by the *Didache* and the *Apostolic
Tradition* of Hippolytus.

Didache VII. 1–3 comprises in the briefest
possible compass the directions as to the rite of
baptism : after the instruction (I–VI) " Baptize
thus : ' In the name of the Father and of the Son
and of the Holy Spirit ' in living water ; but if thou
hast no living water, baptize in other water, and if
thou canst not in cold, then in warm. If thou
hast neither, pour water three times on the head
' In the name of the Father, Son, and Holy Spirit.' "
IX. 5 directs that none shall partake of the Eucharist
" except those who have been baptized in the Lord's
Name." It is clear that the *Didache* contemplates
as normal, baptism by immersion in living water.
An officiant is not specified. As Taylor remarks,[3]
" The instruction to baptize is here given to the
Church or congregation generally, and without

[1] Cf. ii. 38 ; (iii. 19) ; v. 31–32 ; viii. 1–17 ; x. 47–48 ;
xi. 16–17 ; xix. 1–7, etc.
[2] xviii. 24 ff.
[3] *Op. cit.* p. 51

specification of a class of persons by whom the rite is to be administered." We are not here concerned with the "formula" of baptism, a matter of considerable interest to Christian archæology, on which Abrahams [1] has given some illuminating suggestions. It is possible that St. Matt. xxviii. 19 was not regarded in the *Didache* as a baptismal formula, in the way in which it came to be viewed later in Christian tradition, as the discussion below of the Hippolytan rite will indicate. Both in the *Sifra* [2] and in Targ. Jonathan to Lev. xi. 36, as well as in Mikwaoth, appears the prescripton of living water. A concession was made for an old or weak ($\dot{\alpha}\sigma\theta\epsilon\nu\dot{\eta}s$) High Priest on the Day of Atonement to have "warm water poured into the cold (=living) water to take off the chill." [3] For a post-Mishnaic period the Talmud Yer. records the non-success of a petition, in the interest of some Galilean women whose barrenness was supposed to have been due to the use of cold water at *tebilah*,[4] for dispensation from it. The reduction of the quantity of water for the purification of a man polluted by nocturnal emission from a full *tebilah* and immersion, to "the pouring over him of nine *kab* of water" is of the latter part of the first century.[5] So in detail the brief summary given in *Didache* VII. which takes for granted the former section (I.-VI.), a fundamentally Jewish catechumen's instruction, agrees

---

[1] *Studies in Pharisaism and the Gospels*, I. pp. 45–46.
[2] *Mesora* 6 : 3 (Ed. Weiss, Vienna, 1862, p. 77b) ; 'Emor 4 : 7 (Weiss, 96b) ; cf. Erub. 15a ; Hag. 11a ; Pes. 109 ; Yoma 31a.
[3] Yoma III. 5.
[4] Ber. III. 4 and Yer. *ibid*, 6c.
[5] Ber. 22a.

with principles and practice known to current Judaism.

In the year 1910 E. Schwartz published a small work, *Über die pseudo-apostolischen Kirchenordnungen*,[1] the contentions of which [2] were independently advocated and to a very great degree convincingly demonstrated by Dom R. Hugh Connolly in *The So-called Egyptian Church Order and Derived Documents*.[3] Accepting the author's conclusions, so ably presented and cogently argued, we find that in the so-called "Egyptian Church Order" (hereafter *ECO*) we have "in reality the work of Hippolytus," which "dates from the early decades of the third century." [4] The work of Hippolytus thus transmitted is none other than his Ἀποστολικὴ Παράδοσις, *The Apostolic Tradition*.[5] Inasmuch as the somewhat anomalous position of Hippolytus in relation to the ecclesiastical situation of his day would ensure the fact, we may safely regard the *ECO* [6] (=Apostolic Tradition, redacted

[1] No. 6 of the "Schriften der wissenschaftlichen Gesellschaft in Strassburg."

[2] *Ibid.* pp. 25 ff.

[3] *Texts and Studies*, VII. 4, Cambridge, 1916.

[4] Connolly, *op. cit.* p. viii.

[5] *Ibid.* pp. 147–149.

[6] The *ECO* has not survived in the Greek original, but in various Egyptian versions (whence the name with which Achelis, *Die Canones Hippolyti*, *T.U.U.* vi. Leipzig, 1891, p. 26, invests it). These translated texts are to be found as follows : *Ethiopic*, in G. Horner, *The Statutes of the Apostles, or Canones Ecclesiastici*, London, 1904, p. 138, line 11 to p. 162, line 19, and p. 178, line 22 to p. 186, line 8; *Arabic, ibid.* p. 244, line 26 to p. 266, line 11 ; *Coptic (Sahidic), ibid.* p. 306, line 11 to p. 332, line 8. In E. Hauler, *Didascaliæ apostolorum fragmenta veronensia latina, accedunt Canonum qui dicuntur Apostolorum et Agyptiorum reliquiæ*, Leipzig, 1900, are given (p. 101, line 31 to end, p. 211) the Latin fragments of the same text. Connolly (*op.*

A.D. 220– 230) as an authentic document recording the Roman rite of the second century, before the innovatory " reforms " which he so strongly deprecated and sternly repudiated, had been instituted. In short, we possess in the Tannaitic core of the common rite Yeb. 47—*Gĕrim* I. and in the *ECO* roughly contemporary documents of Judaism and Christianity respectively.

It would be difficult exactly to determine in all cases the best readings of the various versions, and still more difficult to ascertain the original, but on the basis of the text given in *Appendix B* (Connolly) it is interesting to note the parallels between the Rabbinic and the early Roman rites. In the brief compass of this present study there is opportunity to call attention only to the more striking likenesses.

1. *The Scrutiny of the Candidate.*—Statutes 28–31 [1] deal with the examination of the prospective converts and " the occupations which they ought to leave off." They are to " be brought to the teachers . . . and they shall ask them for what reason they sought the Faith." [2] Investigation is to be made of their marital life, their character, their occupations : panders, idol-manufacturers, idolaters, soldiers, heathen priests,[3] magicians, heathen officials, adulterers or adulteresses are

cit. pp. 4–6) discusses the relationships between these translations and in *Appendix B*. (*ibid.* pp. 174–194) has made conveniently accessible a continuous text, the Latin fragments being transcribed from Hauler, and Horner's English translation furnishing the body of the material.

[1] Connolly, *op. cit.* pp. 180–182.
[2] Horner, *op. cit.* pp. 147–148.
[3] *Ibid.* pp. 148–149.

all to be rejected. Statute 30 concerns concubines.

2. *The Catechumenate.*—Statute 31 tells us that the normal catechumenate lasts three years, but it may be shortened by good conduct and intelligence.[1] Before baptism (Statute 33) the candidates are to sustain a more searching examination—whether " they lived in the fear of God " and their conduct was marked by acts of charity and philanthropy.[2] " When the day draws near on which they are to be baptized, the bishop binds every one of them by oath, that he may know if they are pure. If one was found that was not pure, they shall put him aside by himself, . . . because it is not proper to baptize an utter alien." A menstruous woman is to be put aside and baptized later. " And they who shall be baptized shall not bring with them any ornament of gold, nor ring or gem of any kind." [3]

3. *The Baptism.*—Statute 34[3] directs that all who are to be baptized shall be " assembled on the Sabbath into one place." Statute 35 reads as follows : " At the time of the cock-crow they shall first pray over the water. And it shall be either such as flows into the font (the Coptic has κολυμβήθρα) or is caused to flow down upon it." Connolly[4] calls attention to the high probability that at this point the *Canons of Hippolytus* and the *Testament of our Lord* may well have preserved a better reading than that given in the Oriental Translations of *ECO.*

[1] Horner, *op. cit.* p. 150.
[2] *Ibid.* p. 151.
[3] *Ibid.* p. 152.
[4] *Op. cit.* pp. 183–184, note 9.

The Canons of Hippolytus XIX. 7 [1] give a reading
which postulates " living " water. It would seem
assured that *CH*, here dependent upon an earlier
text of Hippolytus than that current in the Oriental
Translations known as the *ECO*, read : " Let them
have them to go to the water of a clean and running
stream (?)," or " Let them place them near the water
of the sea (reminiscence of the *O.T.*) prepared with
pure water." The *Testamentum DNJC* [2] has : " In
the following way let them be baptized, when they
come to the water which should be both clean and
flowing." That some such original underlay the
versions is further attested by the context : " This
shall maintain unless there be a scarcity of water,
in which case they may bear water to the tank
after drawing it." [3]

A very striking rubric is that which follows :
" Afterwards all the women shall loose their hair,
and they shall be forbidden to wear their ornaments
and their gold ; and none shall go down having
anything alien with them into the water." [4] That

[1] D. B. Haneberg, *Canones Sancti Hippolyti*, Munich, 1870 :
Arabic text, p. 39 ; translation, p. 75 ; and notes, p. 112. Cf.
Vielhaber, in Achelis' *Untersuchung über unsere Canones* in *T.u.U.*,
Leipzig, 1891, VI. 4, the basis of W. Riedel's edition, in *Die
Kirchenrechtsquellen des Patriarchats Alexandrien*, Leipzig,
1900, p. 211 and notes. Both Riedel and Haneberg seem to
have overlooked the Arabic text of 1 (3) Kings vii. 24, which
may assist in restoring the proper reading now badly perverted
in the *MSS.* ; cf. Haneberg, p. 112, *ad loc.*

[2] Rahmani's edition, Mainz, 1899, pp. 126-127.

[3] Horner, *op. cit.* p. 152.

[4] *Ibid.* pp. 152-153. The parallels and variants are to be
found (Horner) : Arabic, p. 253, and Sahidic, p. 316, and the
original text, Ethiopic, p. 21, and Arabic, p 100. The Sahidic
text is from Lagarde's edition (*Ægyptica*, Göttingen, 1883) of
the MS. Br. Mus. Or. 1320. Haneberg's text of the Canons of
Hippolytus (*op. cit.* xix. 7, pp. 39, 75) reads : *Solvant crinium*

this regulation concerning the presence of anything
alien on the person at baptism is ultimately Jewish
is obvious from a comparison with the Rabbinic
rules in regard to *ḥaṣiṣa*. A "woman may not go
out on Sabbath with a band about her head, nor
can she take the *tebilah* until she has loosed it." [1]
"These things act as 'separation,' (*ḥoṣeṣ*) : woollen
and linen fillets with which women are wont to
plait their hair. But R. Judah said that such do
not act as a 'separation' as the water can reach
the person through them." [2]   Also : " If the woman
keep her hair in her mouth, clench her hand or tightly
compress her lips, it is as if she had not taken her
tebilah as the water cannot come into contact with
every part of her body." [3]   A baraitha further adds
that she may not close either eyes or lips too tightly
or have any foreign substance in her mouth. [4]   The
ground of the prescription is to be found in the words
Lev. xiv. 9 (" Wash his flesh in water," etc.) whence
it is deduced : " in such a way that no separating
element intervene between the water and the
body." [5]   Rogers' [6] suggestion that foreign objects
might be regarded as defiling the water is not the
" reason for ordering their removal " in the case of

---

*nodos, ne cum illis descendat in aquam regenerationis quidquam
peregrinum de spiritibus peregrinis*, which sanctionary reason,
as he points out (p. 112), is lacking in the Syriac and Coptic,
while the former (cf. Rahmani, p. 126) reads : " The bishop is
to see to it that no man wears a ring nor a woman a golden
ornament, since it is not fitting to have anything alien with them
in the water."   (The supplemented form appears in the appendix
to Duchesne, *Christian Worship*², 1904, p. 532, canon 115.)

[1] Sabb. VI. 1.   [2] Mikwaoth, IX. 1.
[3] *Ibid.* VIII. 5.   [4] Nidda, 66.
[5] B. K. 82a, b ; 'Erub. 4a, b.
[6] *J.T.S.* XIII. p. 414.

the Jewish rubric or in that of the earlier text of Hippolytus' rite. Both are obeying the command that the " flesh should be washed," *i.e.* that all the surface of the body be in contact with the water. It is clear that the sanction " lest anything foreign from alien spirits go down into the water " was a later gloss purporting to account for a rubric the key to the purpose of which has been lost.

In the Hippolytan rite immediately after the renunciations follows the anointing with the " mystic oil " (or oil of " thanksgiving "—Coptic). Thereupon the bishop or presbyter, " standing at the water of baptism," witnesses the *traditio symboli*—the imparting of the Creed—performed by the deacon.[1] Thereafter follows the actual baptism : " Then let the catechumen go down into the water, and the priest, placing his hand upon his head, shall question him in these words : ' Dost thou believe in God the Father Almighty ? '[2] And he who shall be baptized shall say thus : ' Yea, I believe,' and holding his hand upon him he baptizes him once. Then shall he say : ' Dost thou believe in Christ Jesus. . . .' etc. ? And when he shall have answered : ' I believe,' let him be again baptized. And again let him say : ' Dost thou believe in the Holy Spirit and the Holy Church and the Resurrection of the Flesh ? ' Let him then say who is being baptized : ' I believe,' and thus let him the third time be baptized. And afterwards when he comes up let him be anointed by the priest with the oil," etc.[3]

---

[1] Horner, *op. cit.* p. 153.
[2] Hauler, *op. cit.* p. 110.
[3] *Ibid.* pp. 110–111.

Two points are of special interest in this description of baptism : (a) There is no " formula " for
baptism in the later sense of the words.   There is a
true summary of belief, acceptance of which and
belief in which is explicitly made by the candidate.
That there are many traces which suggest the
absence of the formula of St. Matthew (xxviii. 19),
or the use of a more primitive and briefer form,
" In the Name of Jesus Christ," persisting in Rome
until a very late date, is well known to students
of liturgics.   (b) The priest's part seems to be con-
fined to retaining his hand on the candidate's head
in the act of baptism.   We have apparently a late
survival of a transitional type midway between
self-baptism and " administered " baptism.   Both
the Hebrew term *tabal* and the Syriac *'amad* are
properly reflexive verbs, used primarily in the middle
voice.   Easton has pointed out [1] that in the received
text of the N.T. only twice is the middle voice
of the verb $\beta a\pi\tau i\zeta\epsilon\iota\nu$ used in regard to Christian
baptism (Acts xxii. 16 and 1 Cor. x. 2), but that in
St. Luke iii. 12, xi. 38, xii. 50 variant (Western)
readings use the middle.   " These readings at least
testify to the passage of the Third Gospel through
a circle which preserved certain early traditions
tenaciously—a fact, of course, familiar in connection
with the abundant evidence of the B text." [2]   " It
is clear that the N.T. preserves traces of a baptismal
practice which differs liturgically from that found
later." [3]

[1] *A.J.T.* XXIV. (October, 1920), pp. 513–518.
[2] *Ibid.* p. 515.
[3] *Ibid.* p. 516.

Before concluding this brief discussion of the Jewish rite of Proselyte-Baptism in its relation to the matured Christian usage, attention must be called to a Rabbinic dictum which is germane to the larger issues of the question. What was conceived to have been effected by the transition over from heathenism to Judaism? Is any change in the individual, so described by the Rabbinic authorities, mentioned which would in any sense be analogous to that wrought by or at baptism, as the initiatory rite, in Christianity?

In four places [1] in the Treatise on Levirate marriage (Yebamoth) of the Babylonian Talmud there is quoted a phrase of very great significance. The earliest name associated with the passage is that of R. Yose ben Ḥalafta, who flourished about the middle of the second century A.D. When the question arose, Why were proselytes so grievously afflicted? R. Ḥananiah explained it as due to their having failed, in the time previous to their conversion, to observe the seven Noachic precepts incumbent upon all men. R. Yose countered this interpretation with the dictum, " A newly converted proselyte is like a newborn child " (Yeb. 48b). In the Tractate Gerim (II. 6) it is R. Judah who adduces much the same statement : the convert is " like a babe one day old." Elsewhere in Yebamoth the same phrase is quoted in connection with the question as to whether the proselyte has fulfilled the command, " Increase and multiply " (Gen. i. 28), with his children begotten before his conversion, and the associated matters concerning inheritance.

[1] Yebamoth 48b, 62a, 22a, 97b ; Bek. 47b.

The argument of Yeb. 62a appears again in Bek. 47b.
Other distinctly legal matters are approached and
solved by reference to the same principle in Yeb. 22a
and 97b. The intricate legal questions developed
by the death of a proselyte without heirs born in
Judaism (summarized conveniently in Gerim III.
8 ff.) have this dictum as their premise.

His conversion affects the proselyte's status in
two respects—towards God and toward God's
people, Israel. After being received as a proselyte
he is regarded as " newly born," with reference to
any guilt as to his past sins and misdeeds, and to
their punishment. This is the Godward relation
of his new status. In regard to Israel, as a child
newly born he is entirely cut off from his family
after the flesh ; all social relations start anew ;
he has a special and peculiar relationship legally
to the fellowship of Israel. This twofold relationship, religious and Godward, legal and manward,
is fully recognized by those who have discussed
the passages.[1] It is a Jewish scholar who sees in
the phrase the evidence that a change of such
momentous consequence was effected by baptism.
" Whatever the real origin of the proselyte's bath

[1] Cf. Strack-Billerbeck, *Kommentar zum N.T. aus Talmud
und Midrasch erläutert*, I. pp. 928–930 ; II. p. 423: " In this
new relationship to God he is now regarded as a newborn child,
free from sin and guilt " ; Stromberg, *Studien zur Theorie und
Praxis der Taufe*, p. 56, note 1, would make the new status of
the convert primarily legal, " in that all former relationships
have been abrogated," yet he would not, like Windisch, limit
it solely to a *kultische Bedeutung* ; Wünsche, *Der babylonische
Talmud*, II. p. 33, note 2 : " The convert has no longer any
blood kindred at all since such relationships were dissolved at
his entrance into Judaism," etc. Cf. Yer. Bikk. 3 (65c), where
Lev. xix. 33, is quoted in the context : " As the proselyte is
forgiven all his sins," etc.

may have been, a baptismal bath was prescribed
for the proselyte to wash off the stain of idolatry."
This "proselyte's bath in living water was to
constitute a rebirth of the former heathen, poetically
expressed in the halakic rule : ' A convert is like
a newborn creature.' The Paulinian idea that
baptism creates a new Adam in place of the old
is but an adaptation of the Pharisaic view. Some
ancient teachers therefore declared the proselyte's
bath more important than circumcision." [1] This
learned scholar's opinion is noteworthy and
significant, but it is difficult to point to a passage
in early Rabbinic literature where the gist of his
contention is anywhere explicitly stated. We have
the verdict that a proselyte is like a newborn child ;
we have the method by which converts were initiated
into Judaism. To the best of my knowledge we
lack, however, the inference that the effect was
wrought by baptism. Such precise deductions are
not in keeping with the way in which the Rabbinic
mind operated, for it is, of course, abundantly clear
that Rabbinic thought would not find this sort of
speculative philosophizing—in the mode of Christian
scholasticism—congenial. It is also abundantly
certain that, as Fiebig has put it,[2] what had to do
with ethics and what concerned the cult lay closely
interwoven in the washings of Rabbinic Judaism,
and that there were " shifting boundaries " [3]
between the two. On the whole, we may affirm

[1] Dr. Kaufmann Kohler, *Jewish Theology*, pp. 414, 417.
[2] F. Fiebig, *Joma*, in *Ausgewählte Mischnatraktaten in
deutschen Übersetzung*, 1905, p. 7 ; *Ethisches und Kultisches
liegt bei solchen Waschungen ineinander.*
[3] Cf. Stromberg, *Studien*, p. 56.

the positive findings of scholars who have treated these texts without espousing their conclusions as to what Rabbinic thought did *not* mean. For example, I cannot agree with Strack-Billerbeck's statement : " This passage does not mean according to R. Yose, that the proselyte by his conversion became a regenerate man from the ethical point of view," etc.,[1] or with Stromberg's comment : " This new birth does not refer to a new ethical state of the proselyte but to his legal status, particularly with reference to the matter of divorce." [2] Verdicts of this sort are both precarious and unjustified : precarious, because we may not regard Rabbinic opinion as a closely articulated system the exact area of which may be so negatively determined, and unjustified, because ethical and " ceremonial " (to attempt a periphrasis for *kultisch*) were so inextricably bound up together that it is impossible to distinguish where one leaves off and the other begins. If the view presented in the first Lecture be at all true, surely we have no right to impose a distinction (and draw deductions therefrom) which was foreign to the mind of our authorities.

At the end of the Mishna Tractate Yoma the following words are ascribed to R. Akiba : " Blessed are ye Israelites, for that ye are cleansed. Who is it who cleanses you ? Your Father in Heaven, as it is said : ' Then will I sprinkle clean water upon you and ye shall be clean ' (Ezek. xxxvi. 25a ; 25b continues : ' from all your filthiness and from all your idols will I cleanse you '). And He says : ' Israel's bath of purification is the Law ' What

[1] *Op. cit.* II. p. 423.   [2] *Op. cit.* p. 123.

does the *mikweh* ? It cleanses the defiled. So the Holy One (Blessed be He) cleanses Israel." [1]

It may be well to summarize the contentions advanced in this Lecture. When in the progress of developing its missionary activity among non-Jews, Judaism had begun to recognize the inconsistency between the theory that the Gentile was unsusceptible to " uncleanness " and the facts, for closer contact and intimate relations with Gentiles were fraught with grave moral dangers, the Rabbis by stigmatizing the Gentile woman as unclean in the degree of menstrual uncleanness, by implication gave sanction to the use of a bath of purification for female Gentiles who wanted to become proselytes to Judaism. Precedent for it was afforded by the code in Leviticus, and the usage grew up naturally and inevitably, beginning possibly earlier but certainly by the second century B.C. In the course of the intervening years before the destruction of the Temple by increasingly restrictive enactments the status of the Gentile was more sharply defined. By 66 he was regarded, officially and authoritatively, as possessing the highest degree of uncleanness. That this ruling was not an act but the consummation of a long continued process, is evident from a consideration of the N.T. documents. The Christian dispensation began with the baptism of John, and the Early Church incorporated the practice borrowed from Judaism. In Jewish and Christian sources of the second century we have evidence by which

[1] Yoma VIII. 9 ; cf. Meinhold's critical edition, pp. 72–73, 80. R. Akiba plays upon the word *mikweh* (Jer. xiv. 8) which may mean " hope " or " bath of purification " (cf. Jer. xvii. 13).

to interpret the silences and the positive date of the earlier literary remains, in two ways : with regard to liturgical practice, and with regard to the legal-theological theory, by then beginning to become explicit and articulate. Our Jewish sources are contained in a Tannaitic reminiscence imbedded in the Babylonian Talmud and in an extra-canonical manual *On Proselytes* (Gerim).

A comparison between the rites there described in bald summary, representing early second-century usage or earlier, and the Christian manuals known as the *Teaching of the Twelve Apostles* and Hippolytus' *Apostolic Tradition*, abundantly justifies the conclusion that all salient elements and many details of the Christian usage may be found in or explained by, Jewish practice. Directions as to the examination, preparation, reception, and baptism of the candidate by immersion are of the same quality and character. There are rubrics common to both rites. The apparently fundamental difficulties of reconciliation seem to be two : the importance of the Christian creed, and the administration of the rite by an officiant. But in the Jewish rite an adequate instruction of the candidate in the fundamental tenets and practices of Judaism is intimated and assumed. Didache I.–VI. undoubtedly represents such a summary instruction. The address of congratulation in Gerim I. 5 is a compend of dogma.[1]   The so-called

---

[1] An analysis of this section (Gerim I. 5, E ; cf. above, p. 35) yields the following dogmatic content : the free choice of the will of man (by which the proselyte elected to become an Israelite) ; the peculiar position of the Children of Israel in the scheme of divine creation ; their unique relationship

baptismal " formula " was not originally regarded as such, but rather as a brief summary of the faith. Secondly, the Christian rite would seem to postulate the existence at one time of self-administered baptism. Even in the rite described in the *Apostolic Tradition* the officiant's part at baptism is scarcely more than that of the official representatives of Judaism in the Jewish rite. It is more than probable that the ancillary Christian usages—anointing with oil, in particular—are derivable from Judaism : the use of oil normally accompanied the bath.[1] It would remain only to inject a new significance into such accompanying developments of the rite at the hands of Christians. The close bond between Baptism and what came to be known as Confirmation may furnish us the clue for the prominent place of the officiant in Christian administration of the two sacraments : if the officiant (in Acts, an Apostle or a direct gift from Heaven of the Spirit)were needed to confer the gift of the Holy Spirit in the second part of the double sacrament, Baptism-Confirmation, his active agency might easily be retroactively posited of the first, the rite of Baptism.

Having considered the liturgical indebtedness of the Christian to the Jewish rite of proselyte-baptism, we find that the verdict on the status of the prosclyte is expressed in the words : " a newly received proselyte is like a newborn child." The thought is old, though its formulation seems to be first attributed to a second-century Rabbi. It

to God and His revelation ; and the doctrine of future retribution and rewards.

[1] Cf. Sabb. IX. 4 ; 41a, 61a; Sotah 11b; Tos. Sabb. III. (IV.) 6, etc.

states a twofold fact : in his relationship to God, now constituted by his conversion to Judaism, he is free from sin, guilt, and punishment so far as concerns the acts of his pre-conversion life ; in his relationship to God's People, the Fellowship of Israel, he is thought of as making a fresh start, a new beginning, entirely severed from all relationships with his past, incorporated as by birth into a new society, beginning life again.   How significant this estimate of the proselyte's status is, and how thoroughly it penetrated every aspect of the rules in regard to proselytes, is of profound importance for the interpretation of characteristically Christian views of the place and function of Christian Baptism. In short, for the interpretation of early Christian belief and practice in regard to Baptism we need look no farther than contemporary Rabbinic Judaism.

LECTURE III

BERAKHA AND EUCHARIST

WHEN Saul was seeking Samuel he was directed to hasten to the high-place, where Samuel could be found, " before he goeth up to the high-place to eat ; for the people will not eat until he come, because he doth bless the sacrifice ; afterwards they that are bidden do eat " (1 Sam. ix. 13). In the passage is latent the whole ancient view in regard to the efficacy of blessings. The early belief might be described as the conviction that the word of blessing (or, for that matter, of cursing) effectively releases divine power, and conveys or exerts a potent declaration of God as to the matter in hand. The importance of the blessing of the father and its final and irrevocable character, is clear from such passages as Gen. xxvii. 7, 35, 37–38; xlviii. 9, 14–22 ; xlix. 26 (cf. Ecclus. iii. 9). The story of Balaam is highly instructive (Num. xxii. 5 ff. ; cf. Mic. vi. 5 ; Neh. xiii. 2), for power was accredited to him who might have wrought evil instead of good, by cursing instead of blessing.

One form of blessing was the grace at meals, according to the principle later expressed in the thought that he who eats or drinks, or enjoys some pleasure of the senses, without offering a blessing, commits the theft of sacrilege since to God belong the earth and all it brings forth, which when consecrated by a blessing it is man's privilege to enjoy.[1] The basis for the thanksgiving-blessing for food is derived from Deut. viii. 10 : " and thou shalt eat and be full, and thou shalt bless the Lord thy God for the good land which He hath given thee." Undoubtedly the release of Divine power in all blessings was understood to be effected by the Invocation of the Name, as in the Aaronic blessing : " And the Lord spake unto Moses saying, Speak unto Aaron and unto his sons, saying, On this wise shall ye bless the children of Israel ; ye shall say unto them : ' The Lord bless thee and keep thee ; the Lord make His face to shine upon thee, and be gracious unto thee ; the Lord lift up His countenance upon thee, and give thee peace.' So shall they *put my name* upon the children of Israel, and I will bless them." [2]

In such an atmosphere as this we of the present world do not find ourselves at home. The idea that a blessing or curse, pronounced by one who possessed proper authority, could be launched off on its mission of good or ill, and that the whole operation lay ultimately in the use of the Divine Name, would seem to be closely akin to what we call magical superstition. As to the facts, interpreted

[1] Ber. 35a, b : " A baraitha reports : . . . R. Akiba said : It is forbidden for a man to taste aught before he have blessed (it)." " The Tannaim ruled : It is forbidden for a man to partake of aught of this present world without a blessing." He who does so is " an embezzler," " is as one who partakes of the sacrifice (committing sacrilege thereby)," "is a robber " of God, etc.

[2] Num. vi. 22–27 ; cf. Rosh Hashanah IV. 5.

psychologically, there can be no question : in a *milieu* where such notions were vigorously alive, phenomena entirely in keeping would undoubtedly thrive, abundantly justifying the hypothesis to those who believed it. What serves, however, to rescue this mass of primitive religious belief from the imputation of magic is the very essential and central element : the use of the Name. As the conception of God developed into a fuller realized monotheism complete in all its implications, so a corrective alignment of the idea of the Name would take its proper place in the whole nexus of religious ideas. The speculations of the Wisdom literature relieved the naïve primitive conception of the burden of its retrograde morality : " as the sparrow in her wandering and the swallow in her flying, so the cause-less curse cometh not (to rest) " (Prov. xxvi. 2). With the affirmation of the existence of the one and only God whose attribute was righteous love, as the objective reality outside the religious con-sciousness of man, the later successors of the prophetic tradition rediscovered the individual : the subjective factor in all liturgical worship and the life of devotion came more and more clearly into cognizance in the years before the Fall of the Temple. What might have survived in a new religious en-vironment as a relic of primitive magic, was reinter-preted in the light of fuller religious development and deprived of all unmoral or unreligious quality.

There remained, into the days of the Second Temple, a wholesome respect and sense of awe for the use of the Name. Possibly in order to prevent the superstitious use of it (perceived by the Rabbis

as a lively danger to Jewish religion) the employment of the Name came to be more and more
restricted and limited. According to Sotah VII. 6
(38a) [1] the priests used the Name only within the
Temple, in accordance with Num. vi. 22 ff.;
outside the sacred precincts the word *Adonai* was
used. On the Day of Atonement the Name was
ten times spoken by the High Priest,[2] but after the
death of " Simeon the Righteous " even this custom
was disallowed and men ceased from pronouncing
it.[3] Sanhedrin X. 1 (cf. 90a) tells us on the authority
of a second-century teacher, Abba Saul, that its
use was prohibited.

Despite this Tannaitic tradition, growing more
strict in the early centuries of the Christian era,
there is good reason to believe that in the period
anterior to this policy of stringent limitation as
to its use, the Name was employed in the blessings
so regularly used in the practice of the religion of
Judaism. The Treatise *On Blessings* (Berakhoth)
shows evidence that corroborates this view, as, for
example, IV. 4. It was the invocation of the
Name [4] which achieved and evoked the blessing it
expressed. Furthermore, throughout the O.T. and
the deutero-canonical literature,[5] the habit of
praying in the form of blessings is abundantly
indicated. In the early Christian centuries many of

[1] Cf. also Exod. xx. 21, in context herewith.
[2] Yoma III. 8 (35b); Tos. Yoma II. 2, Zuckermandel's
edition, p. 183; cf. Yoma 39b.
[3] Yoma 39b; Tos. Sotah XIII. 7, Zuckermandel, p. 319.
[4] " Every blessing must contain a mention of the Name "
(Ber. 40b).
[5] Cf. Kohler s.v. " Benedictions " in *J.E.* III. pp. 8 ff.;
Armitage Robinson in *Theology*, February, 1924, pp. 89 ff.

the extempore blessings employed by Jews were beginning to crystallize into stereotyped forms and their use was gradually being allocated to specified individuals. Thus we find that Tos. Ber. I. 8 inveighs against " those who write down the words of the blessings," despite the fact that such formulations served as the basis for subsequent Tannaitic collections, as in Ber. IX., Ta'anith II., Tos. Ber. VII., etc. By the second century, these blessings were fixed as to form and number, and R. Yose stated that deviations or alterations would render them invalid.[1]

Inasmuch as Judaism knew nothing of a separation of life into the two categories of the secular and the sacred, religion and the common life (at least in ideal) were at all points in contact. The use of the Blessings served thoroughly to saturate the whole round of everyday life with the thought of God, by reiterated reference to whom conduct and action were thus made sacred. As Tertullian expressed it : " Even in the common transactions of life, and of human intercourse at home and in public . . ., God in every possible manner made distinct arrangement, in order that when they (the Jews) encountered these legal instructions, they might not be at any moment out of God's sight " (*adv. Marc.* II. 19).[2] The dignifying of man's relationship to the world of time and space could be

---

[1] Ber. 40b ; Yer. Ber. VI. 2 (10b) ; Ber. IX. 1, 2.
[2] Sed et in ipsis commerciis vitæ et conversatione humanæ domi ac foris, adusque curam vasculorum omniforiam distinxit (Deus) ut istis legalibus disciplinis occurrentibus ubique, ne ullo momento vacarent a Dei respectu.—Tertullian, *Adversus Marcionem*, II. 19.

achieved by means of the realization, quickened constantly through the habitual use of innumerable blessings, of the relationship in which both he and the whole of the world stood toward the Eternal Creator of all. Kohler has made conveniently accessible a tabulation of some scores of blessings in use by Rabbinic Judaism, most of which survive in the present-day practice of Orthodoxy. Several types of such blessings have special pertinence to our inquiry.

The Jewish grace at meals has sustained a long development of which Elbogen [1] treats, and the usages in connection with it may best be studied in the light of a special form, the Common Meal of a Fellowship on the Sabbath Eve. Oesterley has discussed it in relation to the Eucharist [2] and it has received attention recently in the brilliant monographs of Lietzmann [3] and Völker.[4] Accepting Elbogen's historical findings [5] on the evolution of the *Kiddush* (the religious supper ushering in the Sabbath) we may summarize the sequence of the development of the rite as follows : Small groups of friends (*haburoth*) were accustomed to meet weekly for a common religious and social meal, as part of the regular order of their quasi-devotional, quasi-

[1] *Der jüdische Gottesdienst in seiner geschichtlichen Entwicklung*[2], Frankfurt a. M. 1924, pp. 107, 111.

[2] *The Jewish Background of the Christian Liturgy*, Oxford, 1925, pp. 167 ff.

[3] *Messe und Herrenmahl : eine Studie zur Geschichte der Liturgie*, Bonn, 1926, pp. 202 ff.

[4] *Mysterium und Agape : die gemeinsamen Mahlzeiten in der alten Kirche*, Gotha, 1927, pp. 1–11 and *passim*.

[5] " Eingang und Ausgang des Sabbats nach talmudischen Quellen," in *Festschrift zu Israel Lewy's 70 Geburtstag*, ed. Brann and Elbogen, Breslau, 1911, pp. 173–185.

charitable organizations. The information given in
Pes. 102a and in Tos. Ber. V. 2 ff. is to be supplemented by the tradition of e٬ rlier usage for ordinary
occasions given in Yer. Ber. 10d ; Ber. 43a ; Tos.
Ber. IV. 8 (9). According to the principle stated
by R. Akiba that " no one may partake of aught
from this world without a blessing " (Ber. 35a),
at a semi-informal meal when the guests were
seated on *subsellia* or *cathedræ* each said his own
private grace ; when the guests reclined (at a more
formal meal ?) one pronounced the grace for all.[1]
The blessings for bread and wine were invariable
for ordinary occasions : " Blessed art thou, O Lord
our Lord, who bringest forth bread from the earth " ;
" Blessed art thou, O Lord our God, who dost create
the fruit of the vine." [2] The same blessings were
used at the Common Fellowship Meal whenever
observed, as Loeschcke has pointed out,[3] including
the *Kiddush*, which, apparently, in early Christian
and pre-Christian times, was always in private
homes at a meal or banquet : " The *Kiddush* is
observed only on the occasion of a Meal " (Pes. 101a).
The Palestinian custom of the combined Common˙
Fellowship Meal on the Eve of Sabbath comprised :
the beginning of the meal before nightfall, with the
saying of grace, and the greeting of the Sabbath by
means of the special " Cup of Blessing " (כום של ברכה ;
see Sot. 38b), which ushered in the observance of
the Day, signalized also by a special blessing then
recited. The relative positions of these two blessings

[1] Ber. VI. 6.
[2] Ber. VI. 1 ; Tos. Ber. VI. 24 (Zuckermandel ed., pp. 17,
21).
[3] *Z. W. Th.* 54 (1912), pp. 200 f.

(of the Cup, and of the (Sabbath) Day) was disputed by the rival Schools of Hillel and Shammai,[1] which is a convenient datum by which to control the chronological development of the whole institution. Pes. 99b states that a rule attributed to R. Yose ben Halafta (A.D. 150) that the Blessing of the Day follows that of the Cup " maintains for Sabbath eves and the eves of Feasts, but not for Passover." [2] Apparently in Babylonia the *Kiddush*, by the middle of the third century at least, came to be observed in the synagogues, where transient visitors were housed and fed [3] ; while at an earlier date the custom had existed of guests at a Fellowship Meal removing to the synagogue at dusk and returning to their host's home for the Cup of Blessing and the Blessing of the Day (Tos. Ber. V. 3). The ordinary Fellowship Meal included the use of the regular blessings over the bread and wine ; the special *Kiddush* observance, on the eves of Sabbath and Feasts, involved besides a special Cup of Blessing and a special double portion of bread. Loeschcke [4] has noticed some ceremonial objects used in connection with the Kiddush, of which one is a glass cup with the Greek words: λάβε εὐλογία(ν) on it.

These Fellowship Meals were a recognized characteristic of Jewish social life in the Empire, for which explicit sanction was given by the Roman Government, as we learn from Josephus.[5] Rules

---

[1] Ber. VIII. 1 ; Pes. X. 2 ; cf. the debate, *circa* A.D. 150, in Yer. Pes. 37b ; Tos. Ber. V. 2.
[2] Cf. Pes. 107a ; Tos. Ber. V. 2.
[3] R. Samuel, in Pes. 101a.
[4] *Art. cit.* pp. 202 ff.
[5] *Antiquitates Jud.* XIV. 10. 8.

for precedence and for admission to the circle
(*e.g.* Sanh. 63b) were carefully prescribed and
observed. Whenever possible, emphasis was laid
upon the corporate as well as the religious character
of the social life organized in the common meal.
Ber. VI. and VII. prescribe many details bearing
on these principles : for example, two groups,
who may be having a meal under the same roof, are
to say grace together if it is feasible (VII. 5) ;
different forms of blessings and thanks are provided
for different comestibles and viands (VI. *passim*).
The " breaking of the bread " became a liturgical
act,[1] and the symbolic expression in ordinary
parlance for eating a meal.[2] Yet, sacred and
religious as were the Common Meals of the Jews,
it is certain that Keil goes further than the data
warrant when he says, of the home festival of the
Passover-meal, that " the sacrifice has become a
sacrament, the flesh of the offering a means of grace
through which the Lord takes up His redeemed
People into the fellowship of His own House and
imparts to them the food of life for the quickening
of the soul." [3]

We may feel sure that the facts warrant the
following summary : grace at meals consisted in
part of an invariable blessing over the staple food
and drink, bread and wine, which expressly blessed,
not the food, but God who provided the food. The
formula included at one time the use of the potent
Name of God, but in the progress of the years when

---

[1] Krauss, *Talmudische Archäologie* III. p. 51.
[2] *Ibid.* I. p. 104.
[3] *Handbuch der biblische Archäologie*, I. p. 385.

it became invariable, as surrogate for the Name,
the word " Lord " (*Adonai*) became current. The
person as well as the words came to be strictly
regulated by custom grown mandatory. Besides
the common grace at meals, the custom arose
of groups—other than families—meeting together,
especially on occasions significant in the religious
calendar, such as the Eves of Sabbath and Feasts.
These Fellowships or *ḥaburoth* were presumably
extremely common in the religious-social life of the
Jew in the early years of Christianity. It was
entirely in accord with the spirit of Judaism so to
hallow social intercourse, or, to put it the other
way about, to deem social intercourse sacred. The
common meal, with its accompaniment of conversa-
tion on matters of the Law, the administration of
charity, or the religious and spiritual interests of
the company, would so closely approximate what
we should name " sacred " as to suggest an unjustified contrast to " secular." But we have seen that
this antithesis, this dichotomy of life, was alien and
repugnant to Judaism. Sacred and profane,
religious and secular, devotional and worldly, were
never construed as opposites or contrasts. It
remained for the Hellenized mind of Gentile
Christianity so to order and sunder life into
compartments.

But, at the same time, it is important to call
attention to the sense of the necessity of the
blessing. Man has been supplied by God with all
the bountiful provision for his needs. The blessing
which was pronounced upon God not only recognized
and acknowledged man's indebtedness. It also,

so to speak, released the food for man's use. It was sacrilege to partake of God's bounty without pronouncing the blessing of His Name for providing it. All belongs to God, and we share in what is His, when consecrating it by a blessing. No one, as R. Akiba said, must partake of what has not been blessed. Why? The blessing expressed man's gratitude and thanks; it gave him the right to accept what belonged to God and God had given, as by a double ratification: God validates His gift in the act of the recognition by man of his acceptance. The whole relationship, conceived to be enjoined by God, thus precluded the possibility of any contamination or uncleanness, for obedience to the dietary laws, of course, was a prerequisite to the enjoyment of the Divine Bounty.

All these ideas, *mutatis mutandis*, intimately concern the history of the Christian usage in regard to the Eucharist. In order, then, to approach the interpretation of the early Christian practice we may orientate our investigation, incomplete as it must be in the necessities of the case, about the following points: (1) the term *Eucharist* and its significance; (2) the indebtedness of early Christian liturgical practice to Judaism; (3) the underlying theology involved. Under the several topics the relevant material offered by Christian literature of the first two centuries will be considered in roughly chronological order.

(1) The term *Eucharist* in a technical sense seems to have become established by the time of the *Didache* (IX. 1 ff.; X. 1 ff.; XIV. 1, etc.), which document also implies it to be a sacrifice

(*ibid.* XIV. 1, 2, where first appears the significant application of Mal. i. 11 to the Christian Service). In the same source the Church officials are said to "perform the public service" (λειτουργοῦσι, XV. 1), careful restrictions are laid down as to the qualifications of the participants : previous baptism (IX. 5), "holiness" (X. 6), repentance (XIV. 1), proper relationship to the brethren (XIV. 2). In 1 Clement there is mention of the proper officials who are to succeed to the *ministry* and *perform its functions* (λειτουργίαν ; λειτουργήσαντες ; XL. 2, 3), though no specification appears as to the character—whether liturgical, practical, instructional—of this "ministry." "The Eucharist" is technically so used by St. Ignatius (Smyrn. VII. 1 ; Philadelph. IV. ; Smyrn. VIII. 2, 4), who also calls it "the breaking of one bread, which is the medicine of immortality, the antidote against dying" (Eph. xx. 2). Apparently a second synonym for it is the *Agape*, as is implied in Smyrn. VII. 1 : "The heretics absent themselves from Eucharist and prayer, for that they do not confess the Eucharist to be the Flesh of our Saviour Jesus Christ which suffered for our sins and. which the Father, in His kindness, raised up. For those who deny the gift of God, by their disputing come to death. But it would be far better for them to keep the *Agape* (ἀγαπᾶν) in order that they may rise again." Also Smyrn. VIII. 4 suggests that "to make an *Agape*" =to celebrate the Eucharist.

The N.T. precedent for the use of the word Eucharist is abundant. It occurs in the accounts of the Institution, where the aorist participle εὐχαριστήσας seems to be synonymous with εὐλογήσας (cf. Matt. xxvi. 26–27; Mark xiv. 22–23; Luke xxii. 17, 19; 1 Cor. xi. 24–25), and in other passages not necessarily as yet in a technical sense.[1] The question at the outset is, Why was the word Eucharist allocated to this characteristic Christian Rite? The non-Jewish usage [2] affords us entirely inadequate parallels, and does not satisfactorily account for a meaning grown technical in Christianity by the end of the first and the early second century. The subject does not seem to have been discussed in any adequate way by those who have treated the problems connected with early Christian terminology. The word itself, employed in early and widespread Christian sources in a specifically technical sense, points very definitely to the Jewish affiliations and origins of the characteristically Christian service.

The equivalence of εὐλογία and εὐχαριστία, which has been frequently indicated,[3] is interesting testimony to the fact that Greek had difficulties with the Hebrew noun *b'rakha* and the verb. If, for example, one were to translate the Hebrew formula, " Blessed art thou, O Lord," etc. into

[1] The adjective, verb, and noun of the root εὐχαριστεῖν " occur in St. Paul's writings alone of the Apostolic Epistles," as Lightfoot pointed out.

[2] Cf. the evidence of the papyri, in Milligan, *The Vocabulary of the Greek New Testament illustrated from the Papyri and other non-literary sources*, III. 1919, s.v. εὐλογία and verb ; εὐχαριστέω, etc. ; Ramsay in *Expositor*, X. pp. 54 ff. ; Preusschen, *Griechischdeutsches Wörterbuch zu den Schriften des N.T.*, Giessen, 1926. The evidence seems to warrant making εὐλογία= εὐχαριστία.

[3] As *e.g.* Völker, *op. cit.* p. 21 and note 2 ; R. A. Hoffman, *Die Abendmahlsgedanken Jesu Christi*, p. 5.

Greek, it would appear in the words, very familiar
in the Eastern liturgies: Εὐλογητὸς ὁ Θεός, etc.
Inasmuch as the Hebrew form of blessing or benediction was invariably a thanksgiving *to* God *for*
the specific content the formula expressed,
berakha would appear in Greek indifferently as
εὐλογία, *blessing*, or εὐχαριστία, *thanksgiving*.
More congenial to the Greek, however, than the
passive form characteristic of the Hebrew usage,
would be the active : " We give thanks unto thee,
O God." An example of a Greek Christian prayer
to our Lord which is in structure quite like the
Hebrew blessing, may be found in the dying words
of the martyr Carpus: " Blessed art thou, Lord
Jesus Christ, Son of God, who hast deigned even me,
the sinner, worthy of thy lot." [1] The Eucharistic
phraseology of the developed rites of early
Christianity furnishes abundant examples of the use
of the active voice.

If the Prayer of Thanksgiving, which in its
maturer form became the Canon, were the central
portion of the Christian Rite, it is easy to see how
the name *Eucharist* could come to be applied, with
sure and certain inevitability, to the service as a
whole, or to the sacrament of our Lord's Body and
Blood, or to the consecrated Elements themselves.
But the starting point of this series of development
is firmly grounded in the sense that in pronouncing
the blessing over the Elements, the Church was
doing precisely what our Lord did and enjoined,

---

[1] *Martyrium Carpi, Papyli Agathonices* (under Aurelian
161–180 ? or Decian 250 ?), 38; cf. Harnack, *T.u.U.* III. 4
(Leipzig, 1888), pp. 440 ff.

and that the momentous consequences of this obedience ensued by virtue of His ordinance and His power. It was not so much that the great Christian service was a Thanksgiving, but that the Prayer of Blessing, by which was effected what our Lord promised, was itself a Thanksgiving. Hence the nomenclature which rapidly became universal.

Nowhere more clearly than in Justin Martyr does a further fact appear, which justifies and assures this hypothesis. Without attempting, even in outline form, the interpretation of Justin's theory of the Eucharist, attention may be directed to I *Apology*, 65–67, and *Dialogue with Trypho*, 41. There survives in Justin the recollection of a primitive conception in regard to the blessing, which is ultimately grounded in Judaism, that (a) God is blessed for the creatures of bread and wine, which (b) having thus " been thanked upon "[1] " we do not regard as common bread or common drink . . . but are taught that they are the flesh and blood of that very Jesus who had become incarnate."[2] The prayer of blessing is obviously a Thanksgiving to God, as the whole context shows. Yet it is the " thanked-upon " elements which are no longer what they had been before the prayer was said, but have become the Body and Blood of Christ. Justin would seem to make no distinction in terminology between " Thanksgiving " and the Eucharistic prayer. Explicitly and clearly it is the following of our Lord's example who " took bread, *gave thanks*, and said : ' This do in remem-

[1] I *Apol.* 65: 5 (cf. 65: 3, 4) ; 67: 5, 6.
[2] *Ibid.* 66: 2.

F

brance of me. This is my Body,' " [1] and " enjoined " [2] the practice upon Christians.

The same conception of the effective power of
" giving thanks " appears, alongside the later type
—the prayer of direct blessing—in the *ECO* :
" Et tunc jam offeratur oblatio a diaconibus episcopo
et *gratias agat* panem quidem in exemplum, quod
dicit Græcus antitypum, corporis Christi ; calicem
vino mixtum propter antitypum, quod dicit Græcus
similitudinem, sanguinis, quod effusum est pro nobis
qui crediderunt in eum." [3] In the Canon of the
Mass for the Consecration of a Bishop, the narrative
of the Institution, etc., is as follows : " Accipiens
panem *gratias tibi agens* (Christus) dixit : Accipite,
manducate : hoc est corpus meum, quod pro vobis
confringetur. Similiter et calicem dicens : Hic est
sanguis meus, qui pro vobis effunditur ; quando hoc
facitis, meam commemorationem facitis. Memores
igitur mortis et resurrectionis ejus offerimus tibi
panem et calicem *gratias tibi agentes*, quia nos dignos
habuisti adstare coram te et tibi ministrare. . . ." [4]
Immediately after this (in the Latin fragments)
occurs a prayer for direct blessing of oil, introduced
by the words : " Si quis oleum offert, secundum
panis oblationem et vini et non ad sermonem dicat,

---

[1] I *Apol.* 66 : 3.
[2] This would seem to be Justin's sense of παρέδωκεν ; cf.
ibid. 66 : 1 ; *Trypho*, 41 : 1. *Ibid.* 41 : 2 brings in the quotation
from Mal. i. 10 ff., and is preceded by an attempt to discover a
" type " of the Eucharist in the sacrifice of those cleansed from
leprosy. The Eucharist is the sacrifice spoken of by Malachi
(*ibid.* 41 : 3).
[3] At the first Communion of the newly baptized, Hauler,
op. cit. p. 112. Cf. Lietzmann, p. 190 and note 2.
[4] Hauler, *op. cit.* p. 107 ; a Greek translation in Lietzmann,
Messe und Herrenmahl, pp. 174-175.

sed simili virtute *gratias referat* dicens," etc.) and
the blessing of cheese and olives is quite of the later
Latin type : " Sanctify this milk," etc.[1] In the
Ethiopic *ECO* there is a strict distinction between
" the bread of blessing," or *Eulogia*, and " the
oblation as of the Body of our Lord " (Statute 36),[2]
showing that Eucharist and Agape were separated
in fact and distinguished in terminology. Similarly
in the Latin account of the Supper (Agape, probably ;
certainly not the Eucharist) the people are urged
to be prompt in receiving the *benedictionem*
($=\epsilon\dot{v}\lambda o\gamma\dot{\iota}a\nu$) from the hand of the priest or deacon.
" Laicus enim benedictionem facere non potes." [3]

In the light of the Eucharistic prayer in *ECO*
what can be said to be the essential act of the Rite ?
One sentence, the prototype (after the *Didache*) of
all other members of the family, reads : " Being
mindful therefore of His death and resurrection we
offer thee bread and the cup, giving thanks unto
thee, *for that* thou hast regarded us as worthy to
stand before thee and minister unto thee." Thereafter follows the petition " to send the Holy Spirit
upon the oblation of the Holy Church, granting
that all saints may be brought together into one
who receive (It) to be filled with the Holy Spirit
unto the confirmation of the Faith in truth, that
we may praise and glorify Thee through Thy Child
(*per puerum*) Jesus Christ," etc.[4] Lietzmann's
translation into Greek renders the *quia* (English
italicized above) by $\dot{\epsilon}\phi$' $o\hat{\iota}s$. It may well have
represented a simple $\ddot{o}\tau\iota$. The point of the *ECO*

---

[1] Hauler, *op. cit.* pp. 107–108. [2] Horner, *op. cit.* p. 157.
[3] Hauler, *op. cit.* p. 114. [4] *Ibid.* p. 107.

rite lies not in the epiklesis, but in the pronouncement by the proper official, thereunto authorized,
of the words of thanksgiving Certainly, as
Lietzmann has indicated, the " epiklesis " can hardly
be thought of as an implicit and indirect prayer
for the change of the Elements.[1] He has rightly
translated *tibi ministrare* by ἱερατεύειν σοι
(p. 57) : the fulfilment of our Lord's words is
achieved by the use of the Thanksgiving by the due
official, who possesses priestly power.

The discussion [2] of the earliest specific Eucharistic
prayers, those in the *Didache*, has brought out the
resemblances between the prayers over the cup and
the bread (in IX. and X.) and Jewish prototypes,
as well as the striking divergences. Klein has
assembled a mass of Rabbinic material in his article
in the *Zeitschrift für neutestamentlichen Wissenschaft*
(IX. pp. 132 ff.) of which little is relevant, save the
well-known Jewish blessings over bread and wine
in Ber. VI. 1. As Völker has shown, whatever
Jewish material has been incorporated has been
fundamentally reinterpreted and spiritualized :
X. 2, 3 speak of the indwelling of the Holy Name ;
of knowledge, faith, and immortality made known
through Jesus ; of the gift not only of physical
but " spiritual food and drink and eternal life
through Him." [3] Lietzmann calls attention to the

---

[1] *Op. cit.* p. 177 ; cf. the Greek translation, pp. 174–175,
and the separate discussion of the several parts, pp. 42 ff., 57 ff.,
80 ff., 158 ff., and context, pp. 175 ff. Cf. also O. Cassel in
Jahrbuch für Liturgiewissenschaft, IV. pp. 169–178 ; Tyrer, in
J.T.S. xxv. pp. 139–150 ; Connolly, *ibid.* pp. 337–364.

[2] Cf. Lietzmann, *op. cit.* pp. 230–238 ; Völker, *op. cit.*
pp. 105 ff., 125 ff. ; Baumgartner, *Eucharistie und Agape im
Urchristentum*, pp. 216–320 ; *ibid.* in *Z.K.Th.* xxxiii. pp. 62 ff. etc.

[3] *Op. cit.* pp. 106–107.

importance of the mention of the "holy vine of David, thy servant" (IX. 2), referring to Psalm lxxix. (lxxx.), 9–20, which Clement of Alexandria [1] understands as a liturgical phrase, pregnant with transmuted messianism. The mention of "immortality" relates naturally to a liturgical phrase of potent sacramental content, which Ignatius (Ephes. XX. 2) seems to have quoted as such and which appears elsewhere in widely separated liturgical types.[2] How thoroughly interpenetrated with sacramentalism is the *Didache* Rite, despite Baumgartner's judgment that "the prayers of the *Didache* are simply grace at meals, without the slightest reference to the Holy Eucharist," [3] is clear from the weighty evidence of the "Name of God, that is, God's Might, God's Spirit (which) has taken up its dwelling in the communicants by means of the celestial Food,'⁴ the Eucharist.[4] Völker also finds that the elements are "the bearers of salutary power," and interprets the enigmatic phrase : "Above all we thank thee, that ' Thou art mighty ' " (Ps. lxi. 12 (LXX) ; Wis. xi. 24) ; *Did.* X. 4) with reference to the satisfying of the soul (cf. ἐμπλησθῆναι ; X. 1) "with heavenly power, a conspicuous act of divine might." [5] He also comments on the order of the elements : "As in 1 Cor. x. 16 so here (IX. 1) the cup, at least

---

[1] *Quis dives salvetur ?* 29.
[2] Serapion, Anaphora 13 : 15 (cf. Lietzmann, *op. cit.* p. 76) ; Gallic liturgy (quoted *ibid.* p. 96); unedited Berlin papyrus (*ibid.* p. 257, and note 2) ; cf. pp. 235, 257.
[3] *Eucharistie und Agape*, p. 311.
[4] Lietzmann, *op. cit.* p. 235.
[5] *Op. cit.* p. 107 ; Lietzmann regards it as dislocated from its context in this place, *op. cit.* pp. 235–236, and note 1.

in the Prayer, comes first, but from IX. 5 ('let no one *eat or drink* of your Eucharist,' etc.) it is clear that in the distribution the Bread was first. It does not follow that one may deduce therefrom a peculiar type in which the Cup came at the beginning." [1]

If the above summary of the early Christian liturgical evidence be correct, we may look elsewhere than in Jewish precedent and antecedents for the explanation of the widespread and practically universal allocation of the term *Eucharist* to the Christian Sacrifice. " The cup of blessing which we bless " is the " communion of the blood of Christ " [2] because in the exercise of the divinely-enjoined Blessing, which was a Thanksgiving, by the proper fulfilment of the directions laid down by our Lord, there was achieved precisely what His empowering words of blessing expressed :   " This is my Body . . . my Blood." The Blessing of God, or the Thanksgiving to God, for, and over the Elements and what they stood for potentially, made effectual and realized the divine promise expressed by One whom the Church had come to regard as God incarnate. Christological belief is really inseparable from its theology of Christian sacramentalism.

Before indicating some of the theological implications relevant to the interpretation of the early Eucharist, in the light of its Jewish antecedents, it will be necessary to discover what are the affilia-

[1] *Op. cit.* p. 127, note 2. Is a divergence in Jewish usage the basis of the possible variation in the Christian ?
[2] 1 Cor. x. 16.

tions of the liturgical rites of primitive Christendom with contemporary Jewish liturgical usages. How far is the early Christian indebted to the Jewish liturgy ?

(2) Commentators on the N.T. literature have found particular evidence of the influence of contemporary synagogue worship on the structure and phraseology of both Gospels and Epistles. Students of primitive Christian liturgies have for the most part concerned themselves with the Passover *haggadah* as the chief source of early eucharistic developments. Following in this well-worn path are the brief study by Paladini in *Ephemerides Liturgicæ* [1] and Dom Moreau's larger work. [2] The net result of such investigations of this type are, at the most, suggestive, and, at the least, inconclusive. In attempting the following brief survey of the results of a divergent line of investigation we shall confine our attention chiefly to the *Didache*, the *ECO*, the hints in Justin Martyr, and the seventh and eighth books of the *Apostolic Constitutions* (=*A. C.*).

In regard to the *Didache*, supplementing the comments made in the Lecture preceding, a fundamental principle in ordering the investigation into its Jewish affiliations, antecedents, and parallels may be expressed as follows : Jewish models and usage exercised a controlling influence upon the liturgical structure, ideas, and phraseology of this Jewish-Christian document. The divergences, as

---

[1] Vol. 36, Rome (1922), pp. 416–422 : *De primitiva liturgia christiana ejusque necessitudine ad liturgiam judaicam ;* reviewed by Cassel in *J.L.W.* III. p. 165.

[2] *Les liturgies eucharistiques,* pp. 1–247, Brussels, 1924.

Völker points out in his commentary on Baumgartner, are extremely significant : the mould is
Jewish, if the thought be Christian. It is a more
subtle process than direct copying or borrowing.
Judaism seems to be the one religious rival worthy
of attention. When the Christian is directed not
to pray or fast as the hypocrites do (VIII. 2 ; cf.
St. Matt. vi. 5 ; VIII. 1 ; cf. St. Matt. vi. 16), it is
the current practice of Judaism—the " Eighteen
Benedictions " [1] and the institution of Monday and
Thursday as special prayer- and fast-days—that
the writer has in mind.[2] Judaism furnished a
point of departure, or, rather, stood to Christian
practice as that which specifically provoked and
conditioned its reaction, setting the terms in which
its usages were to be formulated.   In the Eucharistic
prayer (XI. 4 ; cf. X. 5) is a section on the gathering
together into one of the scattered elements of the
mystical Body of Christ (cf. 1 Cor. x. 17) which
directly reflects a petition of the *Sh'mone 'Esre*
(The " Eighteen Benedictions ").[3] While in the
concluding portion (X. 6) we undoubtedly possess
a dialogue between celebrant and congregation,[4] it
probably represents an early bit of primitive Judeo-
Christian liturgy, further removed from directly
discernible Jewish sources.

It would be interesting. to discuss the results of
more recent study into the relation between *Agape*

[1] Cf. Lietzmann, *op. cit.* p. 232.

[2] The *ma'amadoth* or " station " days ; cf. similar Christian
term in Hermas, *Simil.* V. 1 ; Clem. Alex. *Strom.* VI. 12, 75 ;
Tertullian, *de Jejun.* 2 and elsewhere.

[3] *Ibid.* p. 235 and note 1 ; cf. Beer's edition of *B'rakhoth*,
p. 20.

[4] *Ibid.* pp. 237–238.

and Eucharist, for which the *ECO* supplies important evidence. Only in passing, however, may we summarize the two views maintained by Lietzmann and Völker. Lietzmann holds that at a very early date the two were inextricably bound up together, that the Agape-Eucharist was a proper meal, that it derived from the Jewish Fellowship Meal, and that for the Eucharist there were originally two types : that of Jerusalem, consisting of bread only, continuing and deriving from the daily Fellowship Meal of Jesus and His disciples, and that of St. Paul, a true Agape-Eucharist, beginning with bread, comprising a true meal, concluding with wine, and commemorating the Last Supper. " Paul is the creator of this second type of the Lord's Supper,"[1] and his characteristic contribution lies in the words : " Do this in remembrance of me." With most of these conclusions Völker is in disagreement : whereas Lietzmann, following Wetter, holds that the Agape-Eucharist was in very early times one unified observance, Völker is convinced that the " Lord's Supper " was not originally a true meal at all, and that the Agape, independent of it, arose only in the second century. He finds that the speculations hitherto urged fail to account for the Agape : it cannot be explained as originally bound up with the Eucharist, nor as due to O.T. or N.T. prototypes and injunctions, nor to Jewish or Hellenistic antecedents.[2] He advances the theory that it arose in Christian usage as an effect of the conflict with Gnosticism, which had developed a common

---

[1] Lietzmann, *op. cit.* p. 255 (cf. § XVI, for summary).
[2] Cf. *op. cit.* pp. v.–vi. 184–197.

Fellowship meal and thereby elicited a counter-
development on the part of the Great Church.[1]
Völker cannot follow Lietzmann in discerning two
original streams of Eucharistic tradition (the
Jerusalemite and the Pauline types), while he is
willing to agree with him as to the infusion of
Hellenistic influences to account for the sacramental and mystical characteristics of developed
eucharistic belief and practice.[2]

It has already been suggested in regard to the
ECO rite of baptism that Jewish models, usages, and
ideas best explain its phenomena, and interpret its
development.   The rite as a whole has only recently
been receiving proper attention, despite its profound
significance.   " Hippolytus in his *Church Order*
preserved for his community the old ritual, which
has thereby been preserved for posterity." [3]   It is
" the model for all known subsequent liturgies.
On it was based the Antiochene Rite of the fourth
century, of which type an authentic exponent
lies before us in the *A. C.* VIII. (and II.).   Thence
evolved the Byzantine rite," that of Jerusalem,
and the sub-families of the Syrian types.   " Despite
the difficulties surrounding the history of the
Western Liturgy . . . an examination of the
phraseology demonstrates that the Hippolytan text
lies at the base of the Roman Canon." [4]   It is
important to turn our attention particularly to two
features of the *ECO* :

[1] Cf. *op. cit.* pp. 197–202.
[2] Völker, *op. cit.* pp. v. 131 ; Lietzmann, *op. cit.* pp. 250–
251, *et passim*.   The latter discerns two liturgical streams :
Didache-Serapion and N.T. (Pauline)-Hippolytus.
[3] Lietzmann, *op. cit.* p. 259.   [4] *Ibid.* pp. 261–262.

(*a*) In the "Lord's Supper" (which is undoubtedly the Agape) the rubrics provide that the bishop " ought not to fast except at the time when all the people fast, for in case they bring that which is proper into the church . . . he shall break his own bread and taste and eat with other believers, who shall receive from the hand of the bishop a piece of delivered bread before they partake.   It is Eulogia . . . the 'bread of blessing,' not the Oblation as of the Lord's Body." [1]   This is found in Statute 36 of Horner's Ethiopic text, [2] in Canon 47 of the Sahidic, [3] and is paralleled elsewhere, as in the Latin fragments of Hauler.   (It may be noted, in passing, that a distinction is drawn between *Eulogia* and *Eucharistia*, originally synonyms but now technically different.)   The Jewish provisions and directions for the person who says grace to partake of the meal are strikingly like this rubric : " He who pronounces the blessing must partake " (Ber. 52a) : " One may not pronounce the blessing for guests at the breaking of bread except he eat with them, though (the father of a family) may do so for members of his household, in order to train them in habits of obedience to the commandments " (R.H. 29b).   The Latin text of the *ECO* supplies the information that such a supper may also be in a private house with the master thereof acting as host.   The bishop is expected to be present, though in his absence priest or deacon

[1] Connolly, p. 187.
[2] *Ibid.* p. 157.
[3] Funk, *Didascalia et Constitutiones Apostol.* II. p. 112 ; cf. Lietzmann, *op. cit.* pp. 183–184 and note, p. 210 ; discussion of interrelated sources in Connolly, *op. cit.* pp. 67–77.

may act. " Let every one be prompt to receive the
Eulogia from the hand of either priest or deacon.
. . . Thou layman canst not make the *Eulogia*
(*facere benedictionem*)."[1]

(*b*) At the " bringing in of lamps at the supper
of the congregation " we have a further supplement
to the observance of the Common or "Lord's
Supper " (Agape ?). In its full form it survives
only in the Ethiopic,[2] which as Connolly has shown [3]
is probably " a genuine part of Eg. C.O., having
been found in this document by the compilers
of *Testamentum* and *A. C.*" At evening, the bishop
being present, the deacon brings in a lamp and the
bishop gives the salutation and dialogue (of the
Preface) omitting " Lift up your hearts," " because
that shall be said at the Oblation." There follows
a prayer of thanksgiving for the light given men
through Jesus. After the supper psalms are said,
and a "mingled cup of the *Prosphora* " is held by the
deacon who recites from the Hallelujah psalms. The
bishop offers the cup, and, after psalms have been
sung, gives thanks over it,[4] and the distribution
of the *Eulogia* (specifically distinguished here, as
above, from the *Eucharist*) takes place.[5] How
completely Jewish is the whole service is obvious.
It is discussed by Lietzmann who adduces the

---

[1] Cf. Connolly, *op. cit.* pp. 187–188, from Hauler, pp. 113–
114.
[2] Cf. Horner, *op. cit.* pp. 160–161 (English translation ; also
in Connolly, pp. 188–189).
[3] *Op. cit.* pp. 111–116.
[4] Probably a mistake for " bread," as Lietzmann suggests,
op. cit. p. 201, note 2.
[5] Cf. discussion in Lietzmann, § XII. *Die Agape* (pp. 197–
211).

texts of the *Kiddush*. The particular and noteworthy feature, however, is the observance connected
with the Light. One of the three special and
detailed duties of the Jewish woman was the
lighting of the Sabbath light. In fact, both accounts
of the admission of a female proselyte (as we saw
above) [1] include particular mention of the kindling
of the Sabbath lamp. So important was it deemed
to be that in Mishna Sabb. II. 6 occurs the following
passage : " For three transgressions women come
to death in childbed : for not having been careful
in regard to the rules of purification, of the separation
of the priest's portion of the dough, and of the
kindling of the light." In the ancient midrash on
Genesis is a rather pessimistic homily on woman's
share in the Fall : woman had shed man's blood,
hence the institution of the laws of purification
(*niddah*) ; woman had brought disgrace on man
who is the *ḥalla* (=priest's portion) of the dough
of creation, hence woman's duties in regard to *ḥalla* ;
upon woman was laid the third obligation of lighting
the lamp, " because she had quenched (the light of)
Adam's soul " (Ber. R. XVII. 14, end).[2]

How early the kindling of the Sabbath light arose
in the domestic observance of the Sabbath it is
difficult to say. It is interesting, however, to find
the Christian observance of the congregational
supper containing the ceremony of the Lamp. Was
it due to a very early conflation of the Sabbath eve
supper and the Lamp-lighting, adopted as a whole

[1] See above, p. 35 ; Gerim I. 4 ; Yeb. 47.
[2] Cf. Mishna Sabb. II. for details as to the rules ; Yer.
Sabb. I. 4 (5b) gives a slightly different version of the above.

by Christian usage ? The transference of an originally domestic service to the place of worship is
amply justified by parallels. The service of the
Lamp-lighting is very old in Christianity, and with
it is associated what is probably the earliest Christian
hymn : Φῶς ἱλαρόν,[1] so popular to-day in the
familiar words : " O Brightness of the Eternal
Father's Face." In fact, there is a reminiscence of
the text of the hymn in the prayer : " we having
therefore finished the length of a day and come to
the beginning of the night." The hymn was already
very ancient by the time of St. Basil, who quotes
it in de Spiritu Sancto XXIX.[2] " That the compiler
of A. C. VIII. had before him a copy of ECO which
contained the passage on the lamp, seems certain."[3]
The Arabic Canons of Hippolytus (XXXII.) specify
Sunday, which detail is lacking elsewhere.[4]

When we come to the study of the Eucharistic
liturgies of early Christendom the Judaistic background appears conspicuously. One of the most
primitive features of the Christian Liturgy is the
Dialogue of the Preface. The constituent elements
of the Dialogue are : (a) 2 Cor. xiii. 13 or, as an
alternative, " The Lord be with you " and the
response : " and with thy spirit " ; (b) the Sursum
corda with its response ; (c) and the Gratias agamus

---

[1] Text in Routh, Reliquiæ Sacræ², Oxford, 1846 ff., III.
p. 515.
[2] The further implications of the passage are discussed by
Connolly, op. cit. pp. 113–115.
[3] Ibid. p. 113 ; cf. A.C. VIII. 35–37.
[4] For a full discussion of the evidence of Tertullian, Clement
of Alexandria, and the Church Orders in regard to the Agape,
cf. Völker, op. cit. 6. " Die Agapen im Zeitalter der Patristik,"
pp. 147–184.

with its response.   Of the three phrases, 2 Cor. xiii.
13 appears in *A.C.* VIII. 12. 4, and the *Dominus
vobiscum* in the *ECO.* Ample O.T. precedent
forms the basis for the latter greeting between
priest and people.[1]   The *Sursum corda*,[2] as has often
been surmised, may be grounded on Lam. iii. 41,
of which the text of the Hebrew, LXX., and other
versions offer no substantial variation : " Let us
lift up our heart(s) upon (our) hands unto God in
heaven."   The fact that the Dialogue of the Preface
is so invariable, and that it is everywhere present in
all types of the matured Liturgy is a sure indication
of its high antiquity and certain evidence that it
belonged to the earliest stratum of Christian worship
when its order became formulated.   Finally the
phrase : " Let us give thanks " is ultimately
Jewish, as is clear from the rules enacted by
Rabbinism in Ber. VII. 3, governing the variations
in phraseology appropriate to different sized
groups.   Dalman [3] has investigated the relevant
material.   For the whole development, in its earliest
stages, Lietzmann points to the end of 2 Cor. (xiii.
12–14) as a Pauline form of introduction to the
Eucharist, comprising as it does the Kiss, the Grace
(to which the congregation could reply " And with
thy spirit "), and implying the immediate transition
to the Eucharist.[4]
   When we turn to the examination of the content

---

[1] Discussed by Cabrol, *Liturgical Prayer : Its History and
Spirit* (tr.) London, 1922, p. 47 ; Leclerq in *Dict. d'archeologie
et de lit.* Paris, 1921, IV. 1387–1388.
   [2] It was known to St. Cyprian, cf. *de Oratione Dominica*, 31.
   [3] *Jesus-Jeschua*, pp. 139 ff.
   [4] *Op. cit.* p. 229 and note.

of the so-called "Preface" of the *A.C.* we need to revise our terminology in the light of Lietzmann's brilliant study. He finds in *A.C.* VIII. 12, 6–27 what he names the *Ante-Sanctus*, and in VIII. 12, 28 ff. a section he calls the *Vere-* or *Post-Sanctus*. For convenience this division and nomenclature will hereafter be employed. The *Ante-Sanctus* comprises the five parts following : (*a*) *Theological* : praise of God the Father and God the Son for the creation of the Angelic Hosts and of the World (§§ 6–8) ; (*b*) *Cosmological* : the Creation of the world (§§ 7–15) ; (*c*) *Anthropological* : the story of Adam (§§ 16–20) ; (*d*) *Historical* : God's benevolence to the Fathers (§§ 21–26) ; (*e*) *Transitional* section, introducing (§ 27) the *Sanctus*. Kohler (in *J.E.* s.v. "Didascalia," IV. 588–594 ; cf. 585–588, and in the *Hebrew Union College Annual*, I. pp. 387 ff.), Bousset, *Eine jüdische Gebetssammlung in siebenter Buch der apostolischen Konstitutionen*,[1] and Perles (in the *Révue des études juives*) [2] have all investigated the Jewish origins of considerable sections of *A.C.*, including the above. The summary findings of these scholars converge to testify, as Lietzmann writes, that "the whole *Ante-Sanctus* . . . is of Jewish origin." [3] The *Kedousha* (=the Sanctus) three times appears in the Jewish Liturgy : (*a*) in the *yoṣer*, (*b*) the *tefilla*, and (*c*) at the end of the morning prayer (*Taḥanunim*), and in it we have the models for the *Ante-Sanctus*, supplemented by Biblical as

---

[1] In *Nachrichten der Gesellschaft der Wissenschaften in Göttingen, phil.-hist. Klasse*, 1915, pp. 435 ff. Cf. Baumstark in *Jahrbuch für Liturgiewissenschaft*, III. (1923), pp. 18–23.
[2] LXXX. (1925), pp. 101–102.
[3] *Op. cit.* p. 132 (cf. pp. 122 ff.).

well as other Jewish services. The second form
constituted a source of debate about the middle of
the second century, as we learn from Tos. Ber. I. 9
(Zuckermandel edition, p. 2). Elbogen discusses the
historical problems concerning the *Kedousha* in his
Jüdische Gottesdienst.[1] There is no question as to
the Jewish origin of the *Ante-Sanctus*, which came
to be incorporated as a whole into the Liturgies of
St. Basil, St. James, and the oriental families.

In comparing with the Liturgy of *A.C.* that of the
ECO we discover two singular phenomena : (1) the
whole *Ante-Sanctus*, (2) as well as the *Sanctus* itself
are lacking. The *Post* or *Vere-Sanctus* is obviously
the source of the parallel derivatory section in
A.C. VIII. 12, 28 ff. The absence of the *Sanctus* is
peculiar. It was certainly known and used by Clem.
Rom. (1 Cor. xxxiv. 5–7), and by another Roman
writer, Tertullian (*de Oratione* 3 : *Cui illa angelorum
circumstantia non cessant dicere : Sanctus*, etc.), as
well as by Clem. Alex. (*Stromata*, VII. 12). Baumstark explains its absence as due to omission in the
course of abbreviating the text,[2] but Lietzmann
indicates evidence of its absence in other western
liturgical texts, concluding his discussion with the
statement : " In the Hippolytan text as we have it
we possess an uncurtailed old Roman formula. . . .
It lacks all those conspicuously Jewish sections of the
A.C. . . . We may conclude that in Hippolytus is

[1] Pp. 61 ff.
[2] *Art. cit.* p. 32. In the same article he argues that the
reduction of the double-phrased form of the Jewish *Kedousha*
brought about the single-phrased Christian form, due to the
omission of Ezek. x. 9. Cabrol, *op. cit.* p. 74, says : " The
Sanctus was not originally at this place."

G

preserved for us the more ancient, purely Christian type of Eucharistic prayer, containing neither the Judæo-Hellenistic Praise of God for His works and deeds towards Israel nor the Sanctus, but confining itself to the Thanksgiving for Redemption through Christ." While the *Sanctus* may well have been taken over from synagogue worship, and used in other Christian services, he contends that " it did not belong to the original substance " of the Eucharistic Liturgy.[1] This conspicuously Christian Eucharistic prayer is Pauline in substance. In the fully developed rite of *A.C.* VIII. we possess a résumé not only of the New, but of the Old Covenant as well, while the *ECO* rite, if Lietzmann's contentions be sound, is specifically and characteristically Christian. The difficulties surrounding any deductions regarding an independence of *ECO* from Jewish models and antecedents are, however, very great. How may we explain the numerous other obvious cases of borrowing from Jewish usages? Why, in the case of *A.C.*, should Jewish models exercise so profound and significant an influence after the middle of the second Christian century, as to allow of a supplementing of the rite and the incorporation therein of substantial portions of Jewish liturgical phrases? The subject demands still further investigation.

It is the more striking that by this time the Eucharistic service as described by Justin Martyr comprised a kind of summary instruction, Bible-reading, and prayer-service, combined with the Eucharist proper. The former, it is usually acknow-

---

[1] *Op. cit.* pp. 164–167.

ledged, is based on synagogal precedent and arche-
types. Justin makes no mention of the 'Sanctus at
the place in his description (1 *Apol.* 65 : 3) where
it would be expected. But in his *Dialogue with
Trypho* (41 : 1) he makes a rapid summary of the
substance of a Eucharistic Thanksgiving which
would suggest not only the Hippolytan, *Post-
Sanctus* but the *Ante-Sanctus* as well. Our evidence
is, however, too scanty to warrant any certainty on
this point. The Clementine section containing the
Sanctus (33–34 : 7) may not have belonged to the
Eucharistic rite, but certainly other sections (*e.g.*
59–61) show strong affiliations with the *A.C. Ante-
Sanctus*, as well as its Jewish prototypes.[1] By the
time of Justin we find the Eucharist celebrated
early in the day and apparently dissevered from any
connection with an *Agape*, or more properly, without
any cognizance of its existence. While " Agape "
was a synonym for Eucharist in the post-Apostolic
Church,[2] in the *ECO* the " Lord's Supper " seems to
mean the *Agape* and is sharply distinguished from
the Eucharist, as we have seen.

(3) For any intelligible understanding of the
conceptions underlying the liturgical terms and
usages, in so large part derived from Judaism, it is
necessary to direct our attention to the implicit
theological and christological ideas involved in
them as part of the Christian tradition. If *lex
orandi* be *lex credendi*, the corollary is the converse :
belief conditions, controls, and to a larger extent

---

[1] Cf. P. Drews, *Untersuchungen über die Clementinische
Liturgie*, 1906.
[2] Völker, *op. cit.* p. 114 and ff.

dictates the form and quality of worship. The more completely the indebtedness of Christianity to Judaism be recognized—in fundamental axioms of religious belief and practice as well as in the incorporation of Jewish conceptions and elements into the liturgy—the more strikingly apparent will be the unique evaluation of the Person, Place, and Office of our Lord. Apart from the latent and implicit recognition of His significance the whole of primitive Eucharistic theology becomes meaningless. If Judaism conditioned the reaction by which Christianity engaged upon a tentative evaluation of its Founder, it is surely significant that at so early a date as the end of the first century the Eucharist was called Sacrifice. The Old Covenant was abrogated with the coming of the New; the new sacrifice took the place of the old sacrifice, which had been displaced and brought to an end. Following the interpretation of *Did.* XIV. 3, where the Eucharist is regarded as foretold by Mal. i. 11, 14, Justin Martyr,[1] Irenæus,[2] and others in the early Church found in the Eucharist the fulfilment of O.T. prophecy and the term of the O.T. sacrificial system.[3] That curious document, the *Didache*, is rendered hopelessly obscure and unintelligible apart from a recognition of the pre-eminent place in it of our Lord as Victim and Priest, in consummating the old and initiating the new order, in which the

[1] *Dial. cum Tryphone,* 41 : 2 ; 117: 7–10.
[2] *Adv. hær.* IV. 17: 1–3.
[3] Cf. 1 Clem. 40: 4 ; 44: 4 ; Völker, *op. cit.* pp. 46 ff. ; to Justin, Tryph. 41 : 1, the offering prescribed in Lev. xiv. 10, for one healed of leprosy, is a " type " of the bread of the Eucharist. On it cf. P. G. Wetter, *Altchristliche Liturgien,* I. pp. 144 ff.

Eucharist was the sacrifice. "The Life and Knowledge" which God has "made known through
Jesus" His "servant" (IX. 3), "the Holy Name
dwelling in our hearts, knowledge, faith, and
immortality" (X. 2), "spiritual food and drink and
eternal life" (X. 3), all of which has been achieved
by Him who is "mighty" (X. 4, 5), all imply a
Christology which, while not fully explicit or self-
conscious, both betrays an "advanced" conception
of our Lord's Person, Work, and Office, and yet
operates in the realm and with the terminology and
idiom of Jewish conceptions. As Lietzmann says,
"God's Name, that is, His Power, His Spirit has
taken up its dwelling in the Communicant by means
of the heavenly food." [1] There is, throughout, every
token of primitive Christianity—even the expecta-
tion of the Parousia (X. 6), which conception has
been transmuted as this hope has been fulfilled
in part sacramentally : *maranatha* in the sense of
"The Lord *has* come."

The sacrifice is constituted of prayer and thanksgiving,[2] for thereby it is achieved. These are the
inevitable and divinely appointed means, on the
human side, for its consummation. The Eucharist
is the peculiar opportunity for the congregation to
thank Him who dispenses all good and perfect gifts,
in praising and honouring Him.[3] This "Thanksgiving" is sacramental. In Ignatius, "more than

---

[1] *Op. cit.* p. 235, and cf. pp. ff.
[2] Cf. Ignatius, Ephes. XIII. 1 ; Justin, *Dialog.* 117 :
"Prayers and Thanksgivings when offered by worthy persons
are alone the complete and divinely approved Oblation."
[3] Völker, *op. cit.* p. 135 ; cf. Did. XIV. 1 ; Justin, 1 Apol.
67: 5.

earthly powers are mediated with the Eucharist, as each believer must receive to himself the Bread and Wine . . . in order thereby to obtain the sure warrant that he shares in eternal life." He would have, the Docetists partake of the Eucharist " in order that they may rise again." [1] In all Ignatius' teaching in regard to eternal life he is not urging any Hellenistic view of the immortality of the soul, but the Jewish doctrine of the Resurrection of the body ; hence his emphasis on the reality of our Lord's human flesh,[2] his opposition to Docetism with its dualistic premises,[3] and his argument based upon rather than converging toward, the actuality [4] of the Eucharistic elements as bearers of Christ's Body and Blood and mediating the Eternal Life vouchsafed by Christ through its participation to the body-soul unity which constitutes man. The Incarnation took place, then, " in order for Him to achieve in His own folk the forgiveness of sins, the annihilation of death and eternal life." In this consists His redemptive work in intimate connection with which stands the Eucharist.[5] The Eucharist is thus in Justin " the commemoration for those who believe in Him of His Incarnation,"[6] yet at the same time it furnishes the believer the means whereby he shares in the work wrought by the Incarnation.

If it be said that the " symbolic " and " sacra-

[1] Völker, op. cit. p. 136 ; cf. Smyrn. VII. 2.
[2] Trall. IX. 1 ; Smyrn. I. 1, 2 ; V. 2 ; VI. 1, etc. Cf. also 1 Clem. 49: 6 ; Barnabas V. 1, 6, 11 ; VI. 7, 14.
[3] Smyrn. II. III. 1–3 ; VII. 1, etc.
[4] " They (=the Docetists) withhold themselves from the Eucharist and Prayer, because they do not acknowledge the Eucharist to be the Flesh of our Saviour Jesus Christ," etc. (Smyrn. VII. 1).
[5] Völker, op. cit. p. 139.　　　[6] Dialog. 70.

mental " views of the Eucharist may be both present in a single writer's work—for example, compare Justin, *Dialogue* 70 and 1 *Apol.* I. 66—it must be remembered, as has often been pointed out, that a " symbol " to the ancient mind *was* in some way what it represented ; unlike our modern view, which would regard a symbol as standing for something which it emphatically is not. The Tertullianic terminology —" likeness," " figure " and " representation " of the Lord's Body as descriptions of the Eucharist (cf. *Adv. Marc.* III. 19 ; IV. 40 ; I. 14)—in no way militates against the *reality* of the Eucharistic Body and Blood (*e.g.* cf. *De Oratione*, 19 ; *Adv. Marc.* V. 8). The same kind of language, with the same meaning, appears in *ECO : tunc . . . offeratur oblatio a diaconibus episcopo et gratias agat panem quidem in exemplum, quod dicit Græcus antitypum, corporis Christi ; calicem vino mixtum propter antitypum, quod dicit Græcus similitudinem, sanguinis.*[1] " Representation " has for us lost the meaning of re-presentation. To our sources that which the Eucharistic Elements stood for and symbolized, they had, in the act of their use to that end, actually become, in the sacramental sense.

Besides the belief in the Sacrifice wrought by our Lord for the sins of the world, the gifts of knowledge and immortality mediated through Him, and

[1] Hauler, *op. cit.* p. 112; Lietzmann, *op. cit.* p. 190 ff., interprets making " the likeness of (His) death " to mean : *den Tod bildlich darstellen*, in the Serapion Liturgy. He goes on to say : " Wenn der Beter nun im Aorist fortfährt . . . so ist damit festgestellt, dass er den Opferakt durch das Niederlegen der Gaben auf den Altar und über ihnen gesprochene ' Eucharistia ' als vollzogen ansieht " (p. 193). The bibliographical notes are extremely valuable.

the linking of the whole to the Eucharist by which
He conveyed these supernatural achievements and
powers, the Eucharist was the bond of union of the
believer with Christ and with the members of the
Fellowship.[1] The heart of the matter is purely
theological : Who was He who instituted the
Eucharist ? Thus the problems of primitive sacramentalism become, ultimately and essentially,
christological.

To summarize the considerations presented
above : the Christian Eucharist became explicitly
sacramental by the implicit recognition of His
significance who, as a Jew, is claimed to have
instituted an observance based on Jewish models.
Jewish precedents, usages, and ideas determined its
form. Christian theology established its meaning,
which in the progressive perception by the corporate
life of the Christian Fellowship, reacted upon and
further developed its objective liturgical character.
That even matured evolution never operated
essentially to alter the type, but in fact tenaciously
preserved the marks of its origin, is a significant fact
as well as an illuminating comment upon the early
history of the Christian Liturgy. He who instituted
the observance of the Breaking of the Bread, gave
thanks over it, and called it His Body. The
Thanksgiving was potent, since He who spake it was
God Incarnate. The Word had pronounced the
words : " This is my Body," and His word of
Blessing effected that which it expressed. The
Eucharist was the Christian Berakha, infinitely

[1] Cf. Didache IX. 4 ; X. 5 ; Ignatius, Phil. IV. ; Justin,
I Apol. 67 : 8 ; *ECO*, " epiklesis," etc.

transcending the customary blessings of Judaism, yet in its ,form modelled upon the Common Fellowship Meal of Jewish groups of friends. " The thanked-upon bread " is no longer common bread, " but has become, as He said, the Body of the Incarnate." The Blessing or Thanksgiving [1] is the true Sacrifice offered by Christians, for by it is consummated the re-presentation of His Body and Blood who was offered once for all upon the Cross. Through the new Sacrifice, the Eucharist, its fruits and benefits are mediated to men. The new priesthood succeeded to the abrogated old priesthood, as to the sacrifice : " Mindful, therefore, of His death and Resurrection we offer thee bread and wine, pronouncing thanksgiving for that thou hast deigned to deem us worthy to stand before Thee and minister to thee." [2] May it not be true that a doctrine of the " conversion " of the elements is to be sought not in the development of the Invocation of the Holy Spirit, nor in the recital of the words of Institution, but in the ancient and primitive conception of the Power of the Name recited in Thanksgiving, in conformity with the precedent and institution of Him who first spake the words ? [3]

---

[1] Cf. Tertullian, *de Orat.* 3, 6, 19, 28 ; *de Idolatria*, 22 ; *ad Scapulam*, 2.

[2] Memores igitur mortis et resurrectionis ejus offerimus tibi panem et calicem gratias tibi agentes quia nos dignos habuisti adstare coram te et tibi ministrare (Hauler, *op. cit.* p. 107 ; cf. Lietzmann's Greek version, *op. cit.* p. 175).

[3] Cf. Oesterley, *op. cit.* pp. 205 ff. ; Völker's discussion of the possibility of an embryonic doctrine of transubstantiation in Justin, 1 Apol. 66 : 3 ; *op. cit.* pp. 141–144. He has collected in a valuable excursus (" Die Kultischen Mahlzeiten in den heidnischen Mysterien," *ibid.* pp. 212–223) the relevant material bearing on heathen meals and the Eucharist.

Of "these five commonly called Sacraments, that is to say, Confirmation, Penance, Orders, Matrimony, and Extreme Unction," it would be well to make some mention. That the exact number seven was fixed upon, and that the enumeration in the Middle Ages comprised these five together with Baptism and the Eucharist, does not preclude the existence of each several rite so denominated with its own perspective of continuous history reaching back to very early days. The sacramental canon of the Eastern and Western Churches was fixed long after the separation of the Lesser Eastern Churches from communion with the Orthodox Church. Yet it is noteworthy that these Lesser Eastern Churches possess the same enumeration and delimitation of the canon of the sacraments; the ancestral line of development is therefore much longer than the span of the past seven centuries.

In early Christianity what has been felicitously termed the Rite of Initiation was actually a three-phased organic unity, including what came later to be called Penance, Baptism as its central and essential feature, and "Confirmation." To this service was normally conjoined the Eucharist, at which the newly incorporated member for the first time shared in the high privilege of his Fellowship. Intimately bound up with the administration of these grace-conveying rites, with the instruction of both catechumens and the Faithful, and with the discipline of the Fellowship, were the proper officials whose authentic status and authoritative commission was imparted by Ordination—the rite later called Holy Order. The sanctification of marriage and of sickness had each its due recognition in the rites later named Matrimony and Unction.

For all of these there are numerous and interesting Jewish affiliations. A discussion of the doctrine of the Holy Spirit, or of the Spirit of the Lord, in Judaism is much too large a subject to be attempted here, even in the baldest summary. In innumerable places definite indications are presented by our evidence which throw light both on the development of the doctrine in early Christianity as well as upon the primitive growth of those rites later defined as Confirmation and Orders. The picture presented by the author of Acts, for example, in the earlier chapters of that book, is of a Spirit-possessed Fellowship (not yet of a Spirit-possessing Community). Leaving to one side the problem of sources, so acutely analysed by Harnack, in Acts ii. 38, we find Peter [1] speaking for the rest of the Apostles in answer to the question of the crowd, What shall we do? in the words: " Repent, and each of you be baptized in the name of Jesus Christ unto forgiveness of your sins, and ye shall receive the gift of the Holy Spirit." This normal sequence is so taken for granted by the author that his own surprise is evident in the selection of such extraordinary methods of its imparting as are recorded in x. 44–48; xi. 15–17; xv. 8–9 (cf. xix. 2–6).[2] The central fact in Pauline preaching is the present

---

[1] Cf. Acts v. 32.

[2] Acts viii. 14–17 may have represented what to the author's mind was the normal procedure; xviii. 24–26, is, of course, a problem, unless verse 26 contains a periphrastic description in the words " expounded unto him the way of God more perfectly."

possession by the Spirit,—so much so that the essential act of faith may well have been the statement that the " Lord is the Spirit." [1]

Possession of the Spirit, the chief attribute of which was prophetic inspiration, seems to be placed in a devotional series of considerable interest by a late second-century Rabbi, Phineas ben Yair : [2] scrupulous adherence to the observance of the rules of bodily purity leads to levitical purity, this to continence, thence to holiness, thence to humility, to abhorrence of sin, devotion to the Holy Spirit, the Resurrection of the Dead, etc. This Jewish belief in the possession of the Spirit in the sense of prophetic inspiration (as in the case of St. Simeon in St. Luke ii. 25) is especially to be noted in all the passages in the early records of Christianity where the Spirit's indwelling was testified by the exercise of prophetic power. Similarly, in the Midrash on Numbers : [3] " In this world certain individuals have prophesied, but in the world to come all Israelites will be prophets " (in accordance with Joel iii. 1, a favourite early Christian text).

More and more striking is it that the early Christian belief as to being possessed by the Spirit, is closely knit up with the transmission and mediation of the gift of the Spirit by properly accredited officials of the Fellowship. The larger problems concerning the whole complex of Christian belief—

[1] Cf. 2 Cor. iii. 17 (i. 22); Phil. ii. 11 ; Gal. iii. 2 ff. (Rom. vi. 3 ff.).
[2] Sota IX. 15.
[3] 15 (180c) XIII.; parallel in Tanḥuma, b'ha'alothekha (210b) (Vienna edition, 1863) ; ibid. mikkes, § 4 (96b). Cf. also Midr. R. to Deut. vi. (203d). The Midrashim are quoted from the Venice edition of 1545.

BERAKHA AND EUCHARIST   101

the conviction that the Church was the "true Israel" (which term plays a most significant note in second-century polemic and controversy), that the Fellowship was as a whole a new priesthood, that the place of the Lord Jesus was unique and *sui generis*, that the nexus of belief and practice sustained rapid and important modification, and the like—form the context in which alone the study of specific phenomena becomes intelligible. At the risk of using an unsatisfactory method, certain striking facts may be set down concerning the Jewish belief as to the communication of the Spirit in, through, and to, properly ordained teachers in Israel.

Two functions of the religious leaders of Judaism —apart from the proper priesthood, which does not seem to be relevant to our discussion—can be distinguished : (*a*) official teaching with the authority of knowledge based on study and acquaintance with the Tradition ; (*b*) disciplinary jurisdiction over cases of conduct taken cognizance of by Biblical or Rabbinic law. The term for the ordination of a scholar, for the period contemporary with that of the early Christian history within our scope, was *semikha*, the "laying on" (of hands). The O.T. precedent was Num. xxvii. 18–23 (and Deut. xxxiv. 9). According to the Rabbinic interpretation[1] of the passage, Moses causes Joshua to sit with him, laid his hands upon him, thereby imparting something of his honour to him, and giving him the

---

[1] Sifre to Numbers (Friedmann, Vilna, 1864) xxvii. 18, § 140 (52b); cf. Sifre zuta to Num. xxvii. 18 ; Midr. R. to Num. xxi. (192a) ; Sifre to Deut. xxxiv. 9, § 357 (150a).

Spirit. The Mishna employs the word *samakh, to ordain* [1] and its related derivatives for " ordinand," " ordainer," " ordination." Ordinands were chosen from the ranks of the " disciples of the scholars " or " learned men " ; the class as a whole, the " wise " (*hakhamim*), comprised only such men as had received ordination. Before the Hadrianic War (A.D. 133) the individual scholar [2] might ordain his own students ; thereafter the process was regulated to provide official cognizance by the *Nasi* and the College of the ordination of new candidates. Of the " scholars " or " sages "—the category of ordained men—one order was of " elders " (*z'kenim*), for whose ordination it was necessary for three sages to act. [3] During the earlier Mishnaic period there is no doubt that ordination took place regularly by laying on hands. Our later evidence [4] is equally clear that ordination by nomination or appointment became the rule. To R. Juda ben Baba (+136) belongs the credit of continuing the line of ordination, so that no link of the chain was broken. This he did at the cost of his life, as the Roman Government had prohibited ordination under stringent penalties. [5] Thus only could the right of pronouncing judgment in cases involving discipline

---

[1] Cf. Sanh. IV. 4.

[2] Thus R. Abba (*circa* 290) in Yer. Sanh. I. (19a), adducing R. Yohanan ben Zakkai (+80) and others of the early generation.

[3] Tos. Sanh. I. 1 (Zuckermandel, p. 414). Marmorstein has given reason to believe that the Jewish " presbyterate " was quite early recognized as such. Büchler makes it probable that the provision of three official witnesses, or two co-ordaining assistants, dates from the Synod of Usha, *circa* 134. The same provision is specified in a baraitha in Sanh. 13b.

[4] *Circa* 280, in Yer. Bikk. III. (65d).

[5] Sanh. 13b–14a ; also in *A. Z.* 8b.

(the second of the two notable functions of official Jewish leaders) be maintained and continued. In this connection the succession of the gift of the Spirit was essential; strangely enough, it was not deemed of so vital importance for the other official function, that of accredited teacher. It seems highly probable that the change from the method of ordaining by laying on hands to that of appellation or nomination took place because Christian had preëmpted the usage, and it had thereby become distinctively Christian.[1]

Elders, properly so ordained, made up both the Great Sanhedrin—on the analogy of the Seventy Elders of Moses in Num. xi. 16—and the local Sanhedrins. They form the model for the Christian presbyterate, which makes its first appearance in the N.T. records, unannounced and unexplained, in Acts xi. 30, significantly enough at Jerusalem. The ordinand for the office of *zaken* (" elder ") in Judaism must be at least forty years of age (according to Sota 22b), and the care about the selection of elders at Jerusalem was especially necessary in order to keep Sadducees out of the Sanhedrin, which precaution was dictated by the circumstances of the times of Alexander Jannai.

Both "apostle" and "deacon" are Hebrew terms. Before the Christian era the pregnant use of the verb *to send* (*shalah*) indicates a technical meaning like the use of ἀποστέλλω in St. Mark vi. 7.[2] The word *shaliah* (*shaluah*) is

---

[1] Lauterbach in *J.E.* IX. 429; Bacher in *MGWJ*, 1894, p. 122; Strack, *Sanhedrin-Makkoth*, p. 13, note 5.

[2] Cf. Gavin, "*Shaliach* and *Apostolos*" in *A.T.R.* (IX. 3), 1927, pp. 250–259.

commonly met with in the sense of deputy, representative, agent, emissary, plenipotentiary. An old Rabbinic maxim is reflected in St. John xiii. 16b : "neither is he that is sent greater than he that sent him " for " he that is sent is like him who sends him " : the emissary is equal in (delegated) authority to him who empowers and sends him.[1] The term *shaliah* was used in many senses : for the official representative of the Sanhedrin ; [2] for the officiant at congregational worship in the Synagogue [3] ; for the representatives and accredited agents of God,[4] as well as in other connections. The atmosphere of Acts ix. 1–2 is entirely in keeping with Jewish procedure : the " letters from the High Priest " would be accrediting testimonials, for which contemporary Hebrew offers a technical parallel, authorizing the venture of an official " emissary " sent off for a particular function. The word " deacon " or " minister " has ample precedent and parallel in Rabbinic literature, and its true congeniality can best be studied in the Semitic Christian milieu of the early Syriac literature.

Our Lord's " disciples " or " apostles " as such would be like the similar members of the student-group of contemporary Rabbis. What as to their successors in the Christian ministry ? In the present state of our knowledge in regard to the development of the Christian ministry, it is difficult

---

[1] Ber. V. 5 ; Mekhilta to Exodus xii. 3 (4b, Weiss' edition, Vienna, 1865) ; *ibid.* xii. 6 (7a) ; Kidd. 41b ; B.K. 113b, and numerous other parallels.

[2] Gittin III. 6 ; Yoma I. 5 (especially interesting), etc.

[3] Ber. V. 5.

[4] B.M. 86b ; Midr. to Psalm lxxviii. § 5 (Buber edition, Vilna, 1891, 173b) ; Kidd. 23b ; Yoma 19a, etc.

to develop the successive stages of its evolution. Kohler, in his article on the *Didascalia*,[1] is of the opinion that both the term *episkopos* and the functions of the "bishop" evolved out of Jewish antecedents. He would make *episkopos* identical with the Hebrew *parnas*, which in turn is a loan-word from Greek—probably from πρόνοος or προνοήτης. With the gradual disappearance of the "charismatic" and the supremacy of the resident ministry in the second century, a unique position was granted the bishops, and the so-called monarchical episcopate became the normal constituent characteristic of the Church hierarchy.[2] How far, even in the second century, Judaism and Christianity reacted upon each other can be seen from such phenomena as the incorporation, before the middle of that century, of the synagogue liturgical framework into the developing liturgy of the Eucharist, and the constant seepage of Jewish conceptions into the Christian tradition where conditions encouraged this process of spiritual osmosis. The most notable instance of the sort is the Persian Sage Aphraates,[3] whose writings show an immense indebtedness to Rabbinic tradition and the whole cast of whose thought testifies to the

---

[1] *J.E.* IV. cols. 588 ff. The whole article is valuable, as the results of an eminent Rabbinical scholar's investigations into the Jewish character of the early Church Orders. Cf. his preceding article on the *Didache* (*ibid.* cols. 585–587).

[2] In all probability this is also Semitic in origin, as the institution seems to have derived from the position of James, "the Lord's brother," passing from Jerusalem, via Antioch, to the Church at large.

[3] While contemporary with Nicæa, his theology is really that of the second century. The dates of his Homilies are 337–345.

absence of a strict barrier between the two faiths. The polemic of the second and third centuries is also interesting : on the Christian side every writer felt bound to have a fling at the Jews. Sometimes such efforts were in the nature of a *tour de force*. Other instances show an acerbity of feeling (which manifestly betrays a sense of kinship not yet obscured) or a passionate protest against Judaism— a token of the suspicion that not yet was Christianity entirely freed of the stigma of its Jewish origins. Singularly enough, the same types of reaction are represented by Jewish writers : the vigorous denunciations of Christianity, laboured indictments of its beliefs, and strenuous assertions that the Jew really did belong to the True Israel constitute one category. Again, as in the case of the giving up of ordination by laying on of hands noted above, the most adequate explanation of which was the influence of Christianity, two other striking testimonies to the dangerous nearness of Christianity to Judaism are offered in the entire waiving of claim to the LXX by Judaism, and in the abandonment of the use of the Ten Commandments in Synagogue worship. The versions of Aquila, Symmachus, and Theodotion supplanted the Septuagint, which came practically to be surrendered to Christianity. While the early history of the Jewish Liturgy allows of no sure precision in analysing its historical development, it would seem certain that the Decalogue, certainly at one time a part of the daily morning worship,[1] was alone of all the Torah held by certain

---

[1] Tamid V. 1.

" heretics " to have been revealed on Mt. Sinai,[1] that these *minim* were Christians, and that for this reason its recitation was abolished.[2] In short, the influence of Judaism on Christianity did not end with the period represented by the N.T. ; rather, subsequent Christian history—up to Nicæa—suggests how strong and continuing must have been the influence of the earlier religion. We may not think of the two religions as so completely sundered as to make unintelligible such facts as the above, both on the Jewish and on the Christian sides.

It is not improper then to look even into Jewish literature of the second and third centuries, if we would rightly ascertain certain aspects of the quality of contemporary Christian institutions. If the development of the Rabbinate after the Bar Kokheba uprising would seem, in a measure, to have belied the previous history of the official teaching office in Judaism, we must yet remember that its history is really all of a piece. More and more did the teaching office supplant that of the administration of discipline, when coercive jurisdiction had been, at least in Palestine, removed from its province. Moral authority retained and maintained its potent sway. In the earlier period, however, the Sages were ordained to administer discipline and act in the legal capacity as judges. The technical terms, represented in St. Matt. xvi. 19 (λύειν and δεῖν) mean in Josephus [3] to " lift " and to " impose " the sentence (of excommunication). They are represented by exact parallels

[1] Ber. 11a.   [2] Yer. Ber. I. (3c).   [3] *Bell. Jud.* I. v. 2.

in Rabbinic Hebrew,[1] which terms possess as well the senses " to declare allowed " and " to pronounce forbidden." This passage and the further text (xviii. 18 and context) together with St. John xx. 23,[2] all bespeak the whole Jewish tenor of the underlying conceptions : authoritative power to exercise not only the teaching but the disciplinary office was conveyed by our Lord, the claim to possess and exercise which prerogative is the more astounding in the light of the thoroughly Jewish character of the texts. The distinction between authoritative declaration, on the basis of intimate knowledge of the case, of guilt or pronouncement of freedom from guilt, and between effective absolution, is essentially a matter of degree and not of kind. The theological development of Christianity, with its fuller recognition of the significance and uniqueness of its Founder's Person, fully explains the sequence of the history of the administration of Penance.

The gradually achieved Christological definiteness of nascent theology explored more deeply the basis, grounds, and quality of the Apostolic Commission. Thereby the functions of the Christian Ministry came to be contrasted with those of the Jewish. He " who spake with authority and not as the Scribes," had empowered men by His Spirit, and this Spirit guided and inspired them. The *agent* in the transaction and observance of the characteristic rites of Christianity came thus to

---

[1] 'asar, and sh'ra' (or hittir). Cf. the parallels, ḳayyav and patur, in Levy or Jastrow's dictionaries.

[2] For copious references and parallels, cf. Strack-Billerbeck, *Kommentar zum N.T. aus Talmud und Midrasch*, Munich, 1922, I. pp. 736–747, 787–794, etc.

assume an importance and significance possessed by neither the official witness at the baptism of a proselyte into Judaism, nor the ordainer at an ordination of a Jewish Elder, nor the Sage as an official expounder of the Law, or administrator of its discipline. The divergence of the ways is nowhere more marked than in the sense of authoritative office which characterized the typical member of the " resident " ministry in the early Church, and the distinction is ultimately and essentially due to theological conviction on the part of Christianity. For the key to the interpretation of the development of sacramentalism is to be found in Christological doctrine and practice.

As was suggested above, it would seem the most adequate explanation of the change from the middle reflexive use of the verb *baptize* to the active-passive (in the early union of Baptism-Confirmation as one connected rite) is through a consideration of the pre-eminent importance of the celebrant or officiant. While the Holy Spirit did come upon men unexpectedly, the gift was, early in our records, regularly and normally communicated from man to man. In a conjoined primitive Baptism and Confirmation the single officiant may have come, at a very early date, to be regarded as the " agent " of Baptism as he was of Confirmation. Still the retention of the middle or reflexive verb in Syriac presents its own problem, not altogether solved by this hypothesis, though the causative forms of the verb (*'amad*) is regularly employed of the agent (="he who baptizes ")

As an instance of the conviction of their authority

in such matters the account of the Council in Acts
xv. is of illustrative significance for the operation
of the Apostolic office of " binding " and " loosing."
There were three " mortal sins " so reckoned by
Rabbinic Judaism—idolatry (or apostasy), adultery,
and murder, and it was incumbent upon the Jew
to be put to death rather than commit any of them.[1]
Singularly enough, the " three-clause " text of this
chapter (omitting " things strangled " in verses
20, 29) fits in remarkably with this Jewish canon.
On critical grounds, however, it would seem prefer-
able to accept the Received Text, in which case two
of the terms are of particular interest : (a) the word
translated " things strangled " is the Greek equiva-
lent for an inclusive technical term embracing two
types of illegal foods of the Jewish law.[2] (b) The
other word to which attention may be drawn is that
translated " fornication."   The term could not bear
this simple sense alone, for surely converts would
be asked to keep the elementary rules of morality.
What it really stands for is the Rabbinic term
meaning " marriage within the forbidden degrees "
or " incest."   The Rabbis knew two tables of forbidden marriages—that of Lev. xviii. 6–18, and a
further extension of the principle due to Rabbinic

---

[1] Cf. the decision at the Council of Lydda (during the
Hadrianic persecution ; cf. B.B. 40b ; Mekhilta to Exodus
xx. 6 (75b)), in Sanh. 74a ; Yer. Sheb. IV. (35a) ; Yer. Sanh.
III. (21b) ; also Sifre to Lev. xviii. 5 (338b).
[2] The 63rd Apostolic Canon rules that a member of the
hierarchy who eats meat with the blood in it, or that slain by a
beast (cf. LXX in Lev. vii. 24 ; xvii. 15, etc.), or what has
died of itself, is to be deposed ; a layman so doing is to be
excommunicated.   The study of the dietary restrictions of the
early Church is the subject of such monographs as K. Böckenhoff,
Das apostolische Speisegesetz. . . ., 1903.

enactment.   In accordance with the purpose stated
in Acts xv. 19 it is certain that " no further burdens "
would mean that the Council would demand the
observance of the forbidden decrees of Leviticus,
but not the extension of the degrees made by
the Rabbis.   The technical use of *porneia* in this
connection is demonstrably certain from this
passage, and throws light on its probable meaning
in St. Matt. v. 32.   The exercise of apostolic
power in a disciplinary question is employed with
a full sense that the authority was really theirs to
use—a further testimony to the independence from
Jewish tradition even when the whole terminology
and problem were, in fact, impregnated with
Judaism.   Further illustration of the exercise of
disciplinary authority is clearly apparent in the
Pauline corpus, of which 1 Cor. v. 4–5 is as instructive as vi. 1–7, where the Corinthian community
is presumed to possess an authoritative resident
power to take cognizance even of civil cases.
The later position of the bishop as indicated
in the Church Orders continues both branches of
his office : as official teacher of the Christian body,
and as administrator of its discipline, even to the
point of managing its charities, settling disputes,
and presiding over its social life !

In regard to matrimony, which only compara-
tively late reached the dignity of a sacrament, the
guiding principle was to be found in the Dominical
words—St. Matt. v. 32 and parallels.   It is due to
the late date at which the rites became fixed that it,
more than any of the others, seems to have gone
further from the Jewish models, for Roman usage

and legal conceptions influenced its character,
saving the scriptural teaching.   It would seem more
than probable that Dr. Lowther Clarke's [1] hypothesis
is correct, and that the Matthean exception (v. 32)
is a Jewish addition, that the word means " incest "
—in the same sense given above for it in the survey
of Acts xv.   The passage would then be intelligible :
incestuous relationships, tolerable by heathen .
custom, would have to be forbidden in the case of
the parties to such a union entering the Church.
There would not then be the question of a " divorce,"
but that of declaration of nullity.

Associated in the early Church Orders with
Baptism, Confirmation (and later with Ordination
also) is the use of oil for unction.   Anointing with
oil or some unguent was early a part of various
Jewish usages : the consecration of a King, and of
a High Priest, and the like solemnities.   The King
was, according to Rabbinic tradition,[2] anointed in
the form of a corona, while the unction of the High
Priest was in the form of the Greek letter χ, probably a late change from the T form indicated in
Ezek. ix. 4.   The anointing of the priest came into
use in the sixth century B.C., and is first mentioned
in Zech. iv. 14.   Besides these solemn unctions two
other uses of oil were common in Judaism—for, or
rather after, the bath,[3] and as a remedy in sickness.[4]
Secure in the confident conviction that they were

---

[1] *Theology*, September, 1927.
[2] Ker. 5b; Hor. 12a.   Cf. Yoma 72b, 73a.
[3] Sabb. IX. 4 ; Yoma VIII. 1 ; Tos. Sabb. III. (IV.) 6 ;
Yer. Ma'as. Sheni II. (53b) ; IX. (12a); Sabb. 41a ; Sota 11b.
Cf. also Ruth iii. 3 ; 2 Sam. xii. 20 ; Ezek. xvi. 9, etc.
[4] Sabb. XIV. 4 ; Tos. Sabb. XII. 12 ; Yer. M'aas. Sheni II.
(53a) ; Yoma 77b ; Yer. Sabb. XIV. (14c).

"kings and priests,"[1] and also because their Master was the Anointed One, the Christian Fellowship would undoubtedly have drawn upon practices which lay ready to hand in Judaism. Though I have not been able to trace an instance of the mention of the use of oil after the proselyte's self-baptism, it would be a natural custom to expect. Once it had become normal it could be invested with meaning by Christian devotion. The use of oil in healing is twice mentioned in the N.T.—St. Mark vi. 13 and St. James v. 14 ff. A case of healing from the supposed ill effects of Christian magic is told as of the beginning of the second century—concerning R Joshua and his nephew, whom he healed by an unction, near Capernaum.[2] The medicinal effect of such use of oil was not distinguished from other salutary consequences of its employment.

CONCLUSION

The elaborate sacramental system, with its intricate liturgical and its ramifying theological developments, which has distinguished Catholic Christendom, derives from Judaism, if within Judaism be included the Person who is called Jesus of Nazareth. Long nourished in Judaism, Christianity began its independent life to go through the centuries bearing always in its most intimate religious observances the certain marks of its beginnings. Two factors explain sacramentalism— Judaism and Jesus. For its initiatory rite and its most solemn and sacred service the Christian Church

[1] Cf. Rev. i. 6, v. 10 ; 1 Pet. ii. 5, 9.
[2] In Midrash to Ecclesiastes i. 8 (Lemberg, 1861, 9a).

felt sure of its Founder's authorization, who had lived as a Jew among Jews. The reception of the Jewish Proselyte included a baptism : Christian Baptism, indebted to this prototype, was invested with new meaning and, in part, refashioned it, yet it has ever preserved the tokens of its origin. Before the sacrifice of Calvary the Jewish Founder of Universal Christianity had His Last Supper with His Disciples, and thereafter ever since He who was a Jew is commemorated by that which was in origin Jewish ; but as He, Jew though He was, was more than a Jew, so far the Eucharist has transcended its ancestry. In the fullest recognition of its indebtedness to Jewish antecedents only can be seen how much more it came to mean. Likewise with the lesser five called Sacraments, Christianity has transformed its inheritance—yet heritage it is nevertheless. The Ministry, with its scope and function of teaching and disciplining, is Jewish in its beginnings—but how much greater, as He who authorized it is perceived to be not a Jew, or The Jew, but God as Man ! At every point the affairs of life are touched by the life of Jesus in health and in sickness, when the mystery of husband and wife receives God's blessing—and again and again emerge the sure tokens of an indebtedness to Judaism, immeasurably transmuted in meaning by His Power who was Jesus the Jew. Nowhere is the indebtedness of Christianity to Judaism more marked than when it is least apparent, for that which has been received over is transubstantiated in meaning, content, and power.

καὶ ὁ Λόγος σάρξ ἐγένετο, καὶ ἐσκήνωσεν ἐν ἡμῖν.

GENERAL INDEX

(The letter *n* indicates that the reference is to be found
in a footnote.)

Abrahams, Israel, 38, 43
Agape, 70, 80 ff., 86
Anrich, H. E., 16 *n.*
Aphraates, 24 *n.*, 105–106
Apostle, 103 ff.
Apostolic Canons, 110 *n.*
— *Constitutions*, 79 ff.
— *Tradition* (of St. Hippolytus),
    40, 42, 44–45, 56, 57

Baptism, of proselytes, 30 ff.
—, rite of baptism of proselytes,
    33–38
—, Christian baptism, 41 ff.
Baptismal " formula," 50
Baptize, 109
Baumgartner (on Eucharist),
    76–77
Benedictions, Jewish, 14, 59,
    68–69
—, at baptism, 36
Berakha and Eucharist, 59–97
" Bind " and " loose," 107 ff.
Blessings, Christian, 71 ff.
Body and soul, in Judaism, 10–11
Bonwetsch, 2
Bousset, W., 3 ff., 13, 88
Brandt, W., 38
" Breaking of the bread," 67
" Bringing in of lamps," 84 ff.
Büchler, 29 f., 32 *n.*

Cabrol, 87, 89

Christology and development of
    Eucharist, 91 ff., 108
Church, the " true Israel," 2,
    101 ff.
Circumcision, 10–17, 32
— of convert, 34
Clean and unclean, 18
" Common " and unclean, 15
Confirmation, 93–101
Connolly, R. H., 44 ff.
" Conversion " of Eucharistic
    elements, 97
Creed, primitive baptismal, 49,
    56
" Cup of Blessing," 65, 66, 78

Dalman, G., 87 *n.*
Day of Atonement, 15, 18, 21,
    43
Deacon, 103 ff.
Decalogue, Jewish use of, dis-
    continued, 106 f.
Didache, 40, 42, 43, 56, 67, 75 ff.,
    92 ff.
Duchesne, L., 48 *n.*

Easton, B. S., 50
Egyptian Church Order, 40–45,
    56 f.
" Eighteen Benedictions," the,
    80
—, Proscriptions," the, 30
Elbogen, 64, 89
Elders, Jewish, 102

INDEX TO BIBLICAL REFERENCES

INDEX TO RABBINIC REFERENCES

PRINTED BY OFFSET IN GREAT BRITAIN BY
BILLING AND SONS LTD., GUILDFORD AND ESHER

LaVergne, TN USA
31 December 2009
168683LV00007B/70/A